Educational Philosophy of
APJ Abdul Kalam

Educational Philosophy of APJ Abdul Kalam

Dr Ajoy Kumar Manna
M.A. (Philosophy), B.Ed, M.Ed., Ph. D.

SHIPRA

₹995, US$ 33.2
ISBN: 978-93-91978-90-7

2024
First Published in India

Educational Philosophy of APJ Abdul Kalam

Published by:
SHIPRA PUBLICATIONS
LG 18-19, Pankaj Central Market
I.P. Ext., Patparganj, Delhi 110092, India
91 11 2223 5152; 96500 28065
info@shiprapublication.com
www.shiprapublication.com

In Memory of

My Mother

Late Gita Rani Manna

Foreword

Prof. APJ Abdul Kalam, a legend, was not just a figure I admired from a distance. I had the honour of meeting him on multiple occasions, both in the prestigious Rashtrapati Bhavan and at his official residence after he stepped down from his office. My interactions with his ISRO colleagues, while serving on education committees, further deepened my understanding of his remarkable character. I significantly benefitted from reading *The Kalam Effect: My Years With The President*, by Sri PM Nair (2011)[1].

Writing a foreword for a book that explores Prof. Kalam's Educational Philosophy is a significant opportunity. I am grateful to Dr Manna and his supervisor, Prof. Nimai Maity, for entrusting me with this task. This book arrives at a time when our society is facing a serious crisis of inspirational deficiency. I commend Dr Manna for his work, which is based on his doctoral research on Swami Vivekananda's and Prof. Kalam's philosophy of education. Prof. Kalam's philosophy and thoughts on education are subjects of great importance and have been extensively researched. Each researcher and commentator brings a unique perspective influenced by their worldview.

Though popularly known as the missile and satellite man, Prof. Kalam's true aspiration was to be recognized as a 'teacher, a professor'. He would fondly administer oaths to his audience whenever he visited an educational institution and addressed students, a practice reminiscent of the oath

---

[1] Nair, P. M. (2011). *The Kalam Effect: My Years with The President.* Harper Collins

ceremonies in ancient Indian educational institutions (Das, 1933)[2]. His desire to be addressed as a 'professor' was officially fulfilled when he was appointed Professor of Technology and Societal Transformation in December 2001 at Anna University, Chennai. This title, however, was short-lived as he assumed the Presidency in July 2002. Yet, the enduring point is his profound respect for teachers and his unwavering desire to be known as a teacher, even during his Presidency. This is a testament to his serious interest in education, which has shaped his educational philosophy.

I have documented my inspiring moments of meeting with him (Mukhopadhyay, 2023) and reproduced them in this book. I first met him at a book-receiving function at Rashtrapati Bhavan. When I was authoring the concept document on EDUSAT (Mukhopadhyay, 1997)[3] commissioned by DECU-ISRO I was advised by Padma Bhushan and eminent scientist Prof. PV Indiresan to consult Prof. Kalam as he 'understands Satellite the best'. During this interaction, I mentioned about my work in rural West Bengal. He was passionate about rural development which is indicated in his PURA project. I made a presentation on our rural development project in and around my village, Udang at his official residence after demitting the office of Presidentship.

As usual, he was unassuming, extraordinarily inquisitive and enthusiastic. He never gave the feeling that we were with the first citizen of India. Maybe that modesty, simplicity and inquisitiveness made him great.

During our discussions, I identified Prof. Kalam as a *Pragmatic Visionary*. In common parlance, these two words look

---

[2] Das, S. K. (1933). *The Educational System of the Ancient Indian Hindus*. New Delhi: Gyan Publishing.

[3] Mukhopadhyay, M. (2023). *Beautiful Moments: Journey of a Village Teacher*. KDP

contradictory. One is either visionary or pragmatic. Vision without pragmatism is wishful thinking and daydreaming. Let me mention three instances to clarify my view of Prof. Kalam's philosophy.

He had the vision of India as a Developed Country by 2020. India's development depends upon rural development. Prof. Kalam and Prof. PV Indiresan conceptualised PURA *(Providing Urban Facilities in Rural Areas)* as the mechanism. I also had several opportunities to discuss PURA with Prof. Indiresan and contribute to conceptual and presentation documents. The fundamental concept of PURA was to provide urban facilities like good schools, hospitals, medical facilities, roads and transport, small-scale production units, etc., so that people in rural clusters can have a comparable quality of life available in urban areas. This will help arrest or reduce urban migration and rural deprivation. PURA was seen as key to making a 'Developed India'. PURA was proposed for a cluster of neighbourhood villages to make the urban facilities justifiable and cost-effective. It needed the collaboration of several ministries, such as rural development, human resource development, transport, small industries, health, etc. It is a different matter that PURA did not succeed as Indian union and state ministries are used to working in silos. Also, unfortunately, the times for Prof. Kalam and Prof. Indiresan were over on this Earth. His pragmatic vision was to develop India through developed rural life and clustering villages as the unit of development through inter-ministerial collaboration and meaningful collective investments.

During my consultative interaction on ISROs' EDUSAT project, when I started explaining the agenda of our meeting about using a dedicated satellite for education, the 'Satellite Man' in his urgency stopped me, advising me not to use satellite for education; instead, he recommended using a cable network. He explained that there is a fraction of a second difference between visual and sound in satellite communication, which children in their innocence may find 'funny'. It may disrupt their learning. Cable Network won't. His urgency and sincerity of expression made me realise his concern for children and their learning much higher than technology – satellite or cable network, or even education in the conventional sense of the term.

During the conversation, he advised me to consult experts and package learning so that "*all my children* score 90 per cent and above to go to the IITs." I noted "*all my children*", as his affiliation and empathy for the children of India. In 'all children scoring 90 per cent marks', he combines Bloom's Mastery Learning, and the USA' Every Student Succeed Act. I also noted his down-to-earth concept of performance in examinations and learning in IITs, reputed institutes with proper learning environments. His vision was for excellent learning experiences for all children. His pragmatic points were packaging learning, necessary examination scores, and firm affiliation and empathy for students.

His simplicity, seamless curiosity, and ability to pocket his ego and official identity made him a great learner revered by all. Borrowing Gandhiji's words, "Prof. Kalam's life was his message and philosophy". We must study and research more to fathom his mind and educational philosophy.

Prof. Marmar Mukhopadhyay
Chairman, Educational Technology and
Management Academy

Preface

Education is the master key to open the avenues of knowledge generation, employment, behavior modification, life skill development and the shaping of individuals and society. The Indian education system has been evolved from the Rig-Vedic age to the contemporary era with the contributions of many educationists. The present education system has been greatly influenced by the contributions of our great teacher, Prof. A. P. J. Abdul Kalam for the development of the potential of individuals and for building a self-reliant nation, leading to supremacy around the globe. As a teacher, Prof. Abdul Kalam has a clear notion about the meaning of education, aims and objectives of education, the concept of teacher, student, teacher-student relationship, methods of teaching and even the Indian core concept of spirituality in relation to science. His concepts not only reflect Idealism, Realism, Optimism, Patriotism, Pragmatism but also Humanism. The National Education Policy 2020 is greatly influenced by the educational philosophy of Prof. Abdul Kalam. His vision could lead India to successfully place the Indian Tricolour on the Moon on 23rd August 2023. Prof. Abdul Kalam was an ocean and with God's grace, the writer has tried to explore just a drop of it in his best of knowledge and effort and with due apologies for any unintentional mistake.

I express my sincere gratitude to Former Prof. Dr Nimai Chand Maiti, University of Calcutta for his motivation, and Prof. Marmar Mukhopadhyay, NIEPA for his valuable suggestions and to share his practical experiences with Prof. Kalam (2003) in this book.

I would like to mention two books whose ideas I found relevant to the theme – *Wings of Fire: An Autobiography* by APJ Abdul Kalam and Arun Tiwari, and *Ignited Minds* by APJ Abdul Kalam. The lectures of Dr A. P. J. Abdul Kalam and articles on him by the educationists have been consulted to enhance the value of this work. I thank them all.

Thanks to my colleagues Mononita Ghosh, Debanjana Bandyopadhyay, Payeli Sarkar, Subrata Das and Arabinda Bhattacharya for their support. I thank my parents for their unceasing encouragement, and I am especially indebted to my wife, daughter and son for their loving support throughout this venture.

Last but not the least, I would like to thank Shipra Publications and all who directly or indirectly have lent their hands to publish the book.

Dr Ajoy Kumar Manna

Contents

List of Abbreviations

ADE	Aeronautical Development Establishment
CWSN	Child with Special Needs
DRDO	Defence Research and Development Organization
EFA	Education for All
FRO	Floor Reaction Orthosis
GEM	Ground Equipment Machine
GSFC	Goddard Space Flight Center
HECL	Higher Education Commission of India
HAL	Hindustan Aeronautics Limited
ISRO	Indian Space Research Organisation
IGMDP	Integrated Guided Missile Development Programme
IEEE	Institute of Electrical and Electronics Engineers
IAF	Indian Air Force
ICT	Information and Communication Technology
IMM	India Millennium Mission
IIM	Indian Institute of Management
ITI	Industrial Training Institute
IT	Information and Communication Technology
KR	Coronary Stent
LRC	Langley Research Centre
MIT	Madras Institute of Technology
MTV	Music Television Channel
MP	Members of Parliament
MLAs	Members of Legislative Assembly
NASA	National Aeronautics and Space Administration
PSLV	Polar Satellite Launch Vehicle
SLV	Satellite Launch Vehicle
TIFAC	Technology Information, Forecasting and Assessment Council

PURA	Provision of Urban Amenities in Rural Areas
PMO	Prime Minister's Office
PC	Personal Computer
RATO	Rocket Assisted Take Off
SAC-C	Scientific Advisor
SAARC	South Asian Association for Regional Cooperation
TVC	Total Viable Count
UNO	United Nations Organisation
UDHR	Universal Declaration of Human Rights
UNESCO	United Nation's Educational Scientific and Cultural Organisation
UNDP	United Nations Development Programme
UNICEF	United Nations Children's Fund
UEE	Universal Elementary Education
USA	United States of America
UK	United Kingdom
USIEF	United States-India Educational Foundation

1

Prof. APJ Abdul Kalam

Brief Life Sketch

Introduction

The life history of Prof. Avul Pakir Jainulabdeen Abdul Kalam (Prof. Abdul Kalam) – childhood, philosophy of life, work strategy, attitudes, willpower, patriotism, and spirituality, are reflected in his autobiography "Wings of Fire", the motivational book "Turning Points" and different speeches and writings by Prof. Abdul Kalam and other prominent authors, research scholars etc.

Life Sketch of Prof. Abdul Kalam – Important Dates

1931, 15th October (Thursday): Born in Rameswaram, Tamil Nadu, India

1950: Admission to St. Joseph College

1954: Obtained B.Sc. degree from St. Joseph's College

1954: Admission to MIT for Aerospace Engineering, Madras

1957: Graduated from MIT, Madras

1958: Joined HAL

1960: Joined DRDO

1963: Went to the USA for a six-month training programme

1963-64: Visited NASA

1964: Joined as Rocket Engineer at the Thumba Equatorial (Trivandrum)

1965: Worked on an expandable rocket project in DRDO

1968: Establishes Indian Rocket Society

1969: Joined ISRO

1972: Joined as project director of SLV-III

1974: Joined Terminal Ballistics Research Laboratory

1976: Death of his father

1979: Failure of SLV-III

1980, 17th July : the success of SLV-III – Placed the Rohini Satellite into the earth's orbit.

1982, 1st June: Joined as director of DRDO for Missile Technology

1983: Joined as chief executive of IGMDP

1985, 16th Sept: Success of Trishul

1988, 25th January: Success of Prithi

1989, 22nd May: The success of Agni

1992-1999: Joined as Chief Scientist Advisor to the Prime Minister

1992: Joined as Scientific advisor of PMO and Director General of DRDO

1993, 20th Sept: Success of PSLV

1998: Developed low-cost "Kalam -Raju Stent." coronary stent

1998: Success of Pokhran-II Nuclear weapons test, Pokhran, Rajasthan

1999: Took charge of Principal Scientific Adviser of the Govt. of India

2001: Rescued from a helicopter crash on the way to Bokaro from Ranchi (Jharkhand)

2002, 25th July: Elected as the 11th President of the Government of India

2009: Awarded from the California Institute of Technology

2003: Nominated for the Youth Icon of the year Award by MTV

2004 Sept: Lecture in Pan-African Parliament, Johannesburg

26th May 2005: Visit to the Swiss Federal Institute of Technology, Zurich

2006, 25th April: Delivered a lecture in the European Parliament

2006: Nominated for the Youth Icon of the year by MTV
2012: Developed a tablet computer – "Kalam Raju Tablet"
2015, 27th July (Monday): Passed away at 6:30 PM due to a cardiac arrest at IIM Shillong, Meghalaya, India, in the moment of delivering a speech.

Birth, Childhood and Student Life

Avul Pakir Jainulabdeen Abdul Kalam was born on 15th October (Thursday) 1931 in a humble middle-class family at Dhanushkodi - Island of Rameswaram, Tamil Nadu, South India. His father, Jainulabdeen Marakayar, was a wooden boat builder who rented boats to local fishermen and carried passengers from Rameswaram temple to Dhanuskodi and back. His mother, Ashiamma, was a housewife. Prof. Abdul Kalamwas the youngest child of his parents. He had three elder brothers, Mohammed Muthu Meera Labbai Maraikayar, Mustafa Kamal, Kasim Mohammed and his only sister Zohara. Prof. Abdul Kalam's family was devout Muslims but broad-minded towards other religions. Prof. Abdul Kalamsaid, "The high priest of Rameswaram temple, Pakshi Lakshmana Sastry, was a very close friend of my father's." (Kalam & Tiwari, 1999, p. 4). As a child Kalam also had Hindu friends. He said, "My friends Ramanada Sastry, Aravindan, and Sivaprakasan were from orthodox Hindu Brahmin families." (Kalam & Tiwari, 1999, p. 8).

Childhood and Student Life

Prof. Abdul Kalam completed his primary education in a panchayat primary school (Saamiyar School of Rameshwaram). Prof. Abdul Kalam started working at an early age to earn money. In his childhood he started to distribute newspapers to contribute to his family's income and pay his school fees. In his own words "Of the straitened circumstances of my schooldays, the odd jobs I did to pay my school fees, and how my decision to become a vegetarian was partly due to my financial constraints as a college student." (Kalam & Tiwari, 1999, Prelude p. xiv). He had a strong desire to learn and a keen interest in mathematics. He said that Shri Sivasubramaniya Iyer was a good teacher at his school. One day his teacher Sivasubramaniya Iyer took Kalam and his classmates to the seashore of Rameshwaram to explain bird flight with practical examples. The teacher showed the flying seabirds and asked the students to observe their flying motion. All the students closely observed that the birds flew in the direction they desired powered by their own life and motivation. All the students understood the whole bird flight dynamics from that practical example. This was the turning point of child Kalam and at that moment he decided his future goal of life to be a flight engineer.

After completing his primary school education, he was admitted to Schwartz High School in Ramanathapuram. There, he was highly inspired by his teachers including Iyadurai Solomon, who advised him to focus on three forces: Desire, Belief and Expectation. In 1950, Prof. Abdul Kalam was admitted to Saint Joseph's College, Tiruchirappalli, affiliated to the University of Madras, and graduated in physics in 1954. In 1954, he moved to Madras (MIT) to study Aeronautical Engineering and became an Aeronautical Engineer in 1957. According to Prof. Abdul Kalam Prof. Sponder taught him technical aerodynamics, Prof. K. A. V. Pandalai taught him aero-structure design and analysis and Prof. Narasingha Rao taught him theoretical aerodynamics, all these helped him achieve a comprehensive knowledge. Finally the child Kalam transformed into Prof. Abdul Kalam – a rocket engineer, missile-man and technologist.

Philosophy of Life

Prof. Abdul Kalam's philosophy of life is guided by the principles of consciousness of mind, social philosophy and developmental psychology. He understood the power of the inner self, sense of identity, and the importance of working for the nation. He thought setbacks and disappointments were part of life. He did not avoid but faced failure. He believed errors are an opportunity to promote innovation and develop new ideas. So he had the good habit of anticipating errors. He focused on being single-minded to achieve success in life. Prof. Abdul Kalam believes that success lies in desire, belief and expectation. He advised us to believe in ourselves (our innate power) and know the direction. He maintained the policy of doing it now. He motivated people to ask questions, seek answers, choose their destiny, and get satisfaction from fulfilling expectations.

He believes one must work with love and enjoyment to achieve the desired goal. So, the best strategy is to handle the crisis with renewed negative to positive energy. He believed in collective wisdom to avoid setbacks and disappointments. His philosophy is optimistic with the correlation between - spiritual and social values. He believes that "difficulties and problems are given by God as an opportunity to grow." (Kalam & Tiwari, 1999, p. 61). When Prof. Abdul Kalam was emotionally disturbed in project SLV-3, he remembered, "Examine me, O Lord and prove me." This proves that one hastodepend on the great force of God.

Professional (Working) Life

Prof. Abdul Kalam said, "I have had the great opportunity and honour of working with three scientific establishments – Space, Defence Research and Atomic Energy" (Kalam & Tiwari, 1999, p. 179). He worked in the fields of Space, Defence, and Atomic Energy with immense success. After passing the aeronautical engineering degree, Prof. Abdul Kalam joined Hindustan Aeronautics Limited (HAL), Bangalore as a trainee, in 1958.

In the year 1960, Prof. Abdul Kalam joined the Aeronautical Development Establishment of the Defence Research and Development Organisation (DRDO) as a scientist and started his career by designing a helicopter for the Indian Army. In 1963-64, he visited NASA's Langley Research Centre (LRC), Goddard Space Flight Centre (GSFC) in Greenbelt, Maryland and Wallops Flight Facility on the Eastern Shore of Virginia. Prof. Abdul Kalam joined India's first indigenous Satellite Launch Vehicle (SLV-III) programme in the Indian Space Research Organisation (ISRO) in 1969 and became the project director in 1972. Prof. Abdul Kalam made a significant contribution as a Project Director to develop India's first indigenous Satellite Launch Vehicle (SLV-III) which successfully injected the Rohini satellite in the near earth orbit on 17th July 1980. It made India to be an exclusive member of the space club. Prof. Abdul Kalam has done a great job for the evolution of ISRO's launch vehicle programme PSLV configuration and got success in 1993.

After working for two decades in ISRO, Prof. Abdul Kalam assumed the position of Chief Executive of the Integrated Guided Missile Development Programme (IGMDP). His grand success was the development and operationalisation of Agni Missiles (22nd May, 1989) - an intermediate range ballistic missile, Prithvi (25th January, 1988) - the tactical (1985) –a surface to surface short range missile, Trishul (16th Sept, 1985)-tactical core surface to air missile. He was connected with Akash – a surface to surface missile and Nag-an anti-tank missile. Prof. Abdul Kalam held the postion of Chief Scientific Adviser to the Prime Minister and Secretary of the Defence Research and Development Organisation (DRDO) from July 1992 to December 1999. He was the Project Coordinator along with R. Chidambaram for the testing phase of the Pokhran-II nuclear tests in the Rajasthan desert on May 11 and 13, 1998. He strongly believed in the slogan 'weapon of peace'. All his contributions to the country made him proud to be an Indian.

Prof. Abdul Kalam developed a very light material called Carbon-Carbon 'Floor Reaction Orthotic' 400 gram calipers for orthopedic use in place of metallic calipers of 4kg. weight. He served the nation as the Principal Scientific Advisor of the Government of India (SAC-C) from November 1999 to November 2001. He also served the nation as the chairman of Technology Information Forecasting and Assessment Council (TIFAC) for the development of the IT industry. On 30th September 200, 1 Dr Abdul Kalam fortunately survived a helicopter accident on his way to Bokaro (Jharkhand) to join a seminar. He believes that the teaching profession in the world is more important for society than any other profession. In 2001, he took a mission of interacting with students to share experiences with them, helping them to ignite their imagination and preparing them to work for a developed India. He worked as a visiting professor at the Indian Institute of Management (Ahmedabad), Indian Institute of Management Indore, Indian Institute of Management Shillong; Chancellor of JSS University (Mysore). He was a professor at Anna University (Chennai) and a visiting faculty at the Indian Institute of Space Science and Technology, Thiruvananthapuram.

From 2002 to 2007, he served as the President of India. In Rashtrapati Bhavan, one day, one of his co-workers had taken permission from Prof. Abdul Kalam to leave early from work to take his kids to a carnival. But for some reason, he could not leave the office on time. When the worker reached his home, his wife told him that Prof. Abdul Kalam had visited their house earlier that evening and had taken their kids to the carnival.

Prof. Abdul Kalam's life was very simple. As the 11th President of India, he moved to Rashtrapati Bhawan and advised to lock all luxurious rooms as he didn't want to use them. He used only a small room as a bedroom and working room. This humble person kept his dining room locked and had his meals on the floor with other staff in his office. He developed the 'Kalam-Raju Tablet' (1998) for rural health development and the low-cost 'Kalam-Raju-stent' (2012) for cardiac treatment. He said, "I say I get happiness when heart patients carry KR coronary stent in their arteries and when the physically handicapped children fitted with the lightweight Floor Reaction Orthosis (FRO) calipers find their difficulties eased somewhat." (Kalam, 2002, p. 15).

Prof. Abdul Kalam established PURA (Provision of Urban Amenities in Rural Areas) for resource mobilization in rural areas to cover 60,000 villages with 750 million people. He inspired the young generation by saying, "I would like to tell the young men and women before me not to lose hope and courage. Success can only come to you by courageous devotion to the task lying in front of you" (Kalam, 2002, p. 43).

Prof. Abdul Kalam created a route map for the India Millennium Mission (IMM) 2020. He visited Cape Town, South Africa, where Nelson Mandela was imprisoned for 26 years and met Nelson Mandela. Nelson Mandela conveyed his leadership qualities and simplicity in his autobiography (Mandela, 1995). Prof. Abdul Kalam also visited the Swiss Federal Institute of Technology, Zurich and the Swiss Government declared 26th May 2005 as Science Day to commemorate his visit. Prof. Abdul Kalam emphasized five important areas to transform India: education and healthcare, agriculture, information and communication, infrastructure and critical technology (Kalam, 2002, p. 67). He prayed for the nation, saying "Aano bhadrah kratavo yenthu vishwathaha.' - 'Let noble thoughts come to us from every side" (Kalam, 2002, p. 87).

Prof. Abdul Kalam wanted to live the rest of his life peacefully and he said, "I wish to live the rest of my life at peace with myself and others. I have no wish to engage in quarrels with others." (Kalam, 2002, p. 85). In 2015, 27th July (Monday), Prof. Abdul Kalam was delivering a lecture at IIM Shillong, Meghalaya. During his lecture, he collapsed with a cardiac arrest and was shifted to Bethany Hospital, where he was declared dead at 6:30 P.M. The last rituals of late Prof. Abdul Kalam were held on 30th July 2015, at Rameshwaram's Pei Karumbhu ground with state honours in the presence of three and a half million people. The Prime minister of India, the Governor of Tamil Nadu and the Chief Ministers of Karnataka, Kerala and Andhra Pradesh joined the rituals. DRDO built the Abdul Kalam memorial at Pei Karumbhu, Rameshwaram. On 27th July 2017 Narendra Damodar Das Modi, the honourable Prime Minister of India, inaugurated the memorial. The UN declared 15th October 2015 (Prof. Abdul Kalam's birth day) as World Students' Day. In 2003 and 2006 he was nominated as an MTV Youth Icon. A Hindi film titled 'I am Dr Abdul Kalam' was made in 2011, showcasing his positive influence on the younger generation.

Prof. Abdul Kalam has written several inspirational books, most notably his autobiography 'Wings of Fire'- motivating Indian youth, 'Guiding Souls: Dialogues on the Purpose of Life'- explores the spiritual side of Dr Abdul Kalam. "India 2020" outlines a plan to develop India into a knowledge superpower and a developed nation by the year 2020. There are many books and e-books available in the market and on websites.

Publications

'India 2020: A Vision for the New Millennium'
– Dr A. P. J. Abdul Kalam and Y.S. Rajan (1998).

'Development in Fluid Mechanics and Space Technology'
– Dr A. P. J. Abdul Kalam and R. Narsimha. (1988)

'Wings of Fire: An Autobiography of Dr A. P. J. Abdul Kalam'
– Dr A. P. J. Abdul Kalam and Arun K. Tiwari (1999).

'Ignited Minds: Unleashing the Power within India'
– Dr A. P. J. Abdul Kalam (2002).

'Scientist to President'
– Dr A. P. J. Abdul Kalam (2003).

'India-my-dream'
– Dr A. P. J. Abdul Kalam (2004)

'The Luminous Sparks: A biography in verse and colours'
– Dr A. P. J. Abdul Kalam (2004)

'Envisioning an Empowered Nation: Technology for Societal Transformation'
– Dr A. P. J. Abdul Kalam and A. Sivathanu Pillai (2004).

'Guiding Souls: Dialogues on the Purpose of Life'
– Dr A. P. J. Abdul Kalam, Arun K. Tiwari (2005).

'Mission India: A vision for Indian youth'
– Dr A. P. J. Abdul Kalam and Y. S. Rajan (2005)

'Children Ask Kalam'
– Dr A. P. J. Abdul Kalam (2006)

'Indomitable Spirit'
– Dr A. P. J. Abdul Kalam (2007)

'You are born to blossom'
– Dr A. P. J. Abdul Kalam and Arun K Tiwari (2008)

'The Family and the Nation'
– Dr A. P. J. Abdul Kalam with Acharya Mahapragya (2008)

'Spirit of India: Reflecting the concerns, aspirations and dreams of the Indian youth'
– Dr A. P. J. Abdul Kalam (2010)

'The Scientific Indian: A Twenty-first Century Guide to the World around Us'
– Dr A. P. J. Abdul Kalam and Y. S. Rajan (2010)

'Jeevan Vriksh (In Hindi)'
– Dr A. P. J. Abdul Kalam (2011)

'Failure to Success'
– Dr A. P. J. Abdul Kalam and Arun K. Tiwari (2011)

'Target 3 Billion PURA: Innovative Solutions towards Sustainable Development'
– Dr A. P. J. Abdul Kalam and Srijan Pal Singh (2011)

'You are unique: Scale New Heights by thoughts and actions'
– Dr A. P. J. Abdul Kalam (2012)

'Turning Point: A Journey through Challenges'
– Dr A. P. J. Abdul Kalam (2012)

'My Journey: Transforming Dreams into Action'
– Dr A. P. J. Abdul Kalam (2013)

'Beyond 2020'
– Dr A. P. J. Abdul Kalam (2014)

'The Righteous Life'
– Dr A. P. J. Abdul Kalam (2014)

'Inspiring Thoughts'
– Dr A. P. J. Abdul Kalam (2014)

'Governance for Growth in India'
– Dr A. P. J. Abdul Kalam (2014)

'Reignited'
– Dr A. P. J. Abdul Kalam and Srijan Pal Singh (2015)

'Advantage India: From challenges to opportunity'
– Dr A. P. J. Abdul Kalam and Srijan Pal Singh (2015)

Turning Points

1. Appointment as a Senior Scientific Assistant at DRDO, in 1960.
2. Joining as project director of ISRO in 1972.
3. Success of SLV-III in 1980
4. Success of Agni in 1989
5. Taking charge as the Chief Scientific Adviser of the Prime Minister in 1992.
6. Introducing the nuclear test in 1998.

7. Taking charge of the Principal Scientific Adviser of the Govt. of India, in 1999.
8. Rescue from a helicopter accident on the way to Bokaro, Jharkhand, in 2001.
9. Taking charge as the President of India (2002-2007).

Success of Prof. Abdul Kalam

i) SLV-III on 18th July 1980, placed Rohini satellite near the Earth orbit,
ii) Agni Missile successfully launched on 22nd May 1989.
iii) Success of Pokhran Nuclear power test in May 1998.
iv) Development of Tablet computer in 1998.
v) Development of Kalam-Raju stent in 2012.

It is stated that, in response to a question- "What has given you happiness in your life in the last forty years?" Prof. Abdul Kalam replied "I get happiness when heart patients carry KR coronary stents in their arteries and when physically handicapped children fitted with the lightweight Floor Reaction Orthosis (FRO) calipers find their difficulties eased somewhat." (Kalam, 2002, p. 15).

Proud Moments for Prof. Abdul Kalam

Prof. Abdul Kalam was honoured with the Padma Bhushan in 1981 for his immense work in space research (ISRO) and honoured with the Padma Vibhushan in 1990 for valuable contributions to scientific research and the modernization of defence technology (DRDO). He was awarded the Bharat Ratna in 1997 by the Govt. of India. He is the third president of India who was awarded Bharat Ratna after Sarvepalli Radhakrishnan and Zakir Hussain. Prof. Abdul Kalam received honorary doctorates from 40 universities in India and abroad. He also received the 13th Indira Gandhi Award for National Integration from Congress President Sonia Gandhi. On 9th August 1996, Prof. Abdul Kalam received the G. M. Modi Award for achievement in science. Dr Abdul Kalam was chosen to receive the prestigious 2008 Hoover Medal for his outstanding public service. Prof. Abdul Kalam also received the Wernher von Braun Memorial Award from Mark Hopkins at ISDC in 2013. In addition to these awards, Prof. Abdul Kalam also received the Dr Biren Roy Space Award, Om Prakash Bhasin Award, National Nehru Award and Aryabhata Award.

List of Awards and Honours

Year of Award/ Honour	*Name of Award or Honour*	*Awarding Organisation*
2014	Doctor of Science	Edinbergh University (U.K.)
2014	Doctor of Science	Edinbergh University (U.K.)
2013	Von Braun Award	National Space Society
2012	Doctor of Laws (Honoris Causa)	Simon Fraser University
2011	IEEE Honorary Membership	IEEE
2010	Doctor of Engineering	University of Waterloo
2009	Hoover Medal	ASME Foundation, USA
2009	Honorary Doctorate	Oakland University
2009	International von Karman	Wings Award California Institute of Technology, U.S.A.
2009.	Doctor of Engineering	(Honoris Caus Nanyang Technological University, Singapore
2007	King Charles II Medal	Royal Society, U.K
2007	Honorary Doctorate of Science	University of Wolverhampton, U.K
2000	Ramanujan Award	Alwars Rearch Centre, Chennai
1998	Veer Savarkar Award	Government of India
1997	Indira Gandhi Award for National Integration	Government of India

Year of Award/ Honour	*Name of Award or Honour*	*Awarding Organisation*
1997	Bharat Ratna	Government of India
1995	Distinguished Fellow	National Academy of Medical Science
1994	Distinguished Fellow	Institute of Directors (India)
1990	Padma Vibhushan	Government of India
1990	Doctor of Science	Jadavpur University
1981	Padma Bhushan	Government of India

So, Prof. Abdul Kalam is not only a consistent learner but also a consistent performer. His journey of life with desire, belief, expectation and determination is a live illustration for the new generation. It is said, "He had tremendous vitality and obviously received immense pleasure from the world of ideas. His conversation was not always easy to follow but was always fresh and stimulating." (Kalam & Tiwari, 1999, Back Cover Page). "He has an intuitive rapport with the humblest and simplest people, an indication of his own simplicity and innate spirituality." (Kalam & Tiwari, 1999, Prelude p. ix).

Summary

Prof. Avul Pakir Jainulabdeen Abdul Kalam, son of Jainulabdeen Marakayar and Ashiamma was born into a poor fisherman family on 15th October, Thursday, 1931 at Dhanushkodi, Rameswaram, Tamil Nadu, South India. His student life started in a panchayat primary school and in childhood started to earn by distributing newspapers to contribute to his family's income. He completed his school education at Schwartz High School, Rammanathapuram, graduated in physics in 1954 from Saint Joseph's College, Tiruchirappalli under the University of Madras and became an Aeronautical Engineer in 1957 from MIT Madras. In 1958 Prof. Abdul Kalam joined HAL (Hindustan Aeronautics Limited), Bangalore as a trainee engineer. In 1960, he joined DRDO. In 1963-64, he visited NASA. In 1979 he faced failure in SLV-III but in July 1980 he became successful by placing the Rohini Satelite near Earth's orbit. He joined IGMDP and became successful in the Prithi, Trishul, Akash, Nag and Agni missiles and was hailed as the 'Missile Man'. From 1992-1999, he served as the Chief Scientific Advisor to the Prime Minister and Secretary of Defence Research. India became successful in Pokhran II nuclear test on May 11th and 13th in 1998 under his guidance and supervision. He developed light material Carbon-Carbon for orthopedic use in place of metallic calipers of 4 kg. weight, Kalam-Raju Tablet Computer (PC), Kalam-Raju Stent for Cardiatic use. He loved to play the Veena, read books, and to spent time among children. He loved to teach and wanted to be remembered as a teacher after his demise. From 2002-2007 he served the nation as the President of India. He laid emphasis on education and health care, agriculture, information and communication, infrastructure and critical technology. He established PURA for the mobilization of resources in rural areas.

On 27th July 2015 he passed away at IIM Shillong, Meghalaya, when he was delivering lecture to students. He wrote a number of books, poem and was awarded with Padma Bhusan, Padma Bibhusan, Bharat Ratna and honorary doctorate degrees from more than 35 universities. Prof. Abdul Kalam inspired youth to see dream and to fulfill it. It is said about Prof. Abdul Kalam, "He had tremendous vitality and obviously received immense pleasure from the world of ideas. His conversation was not always easy to follow but was always fresh and stimulating." (Kalam & Tiwari, 1999, Preface p. ix).

2

Development of Indian Education System

"Om Asato Maa Sad-Gamaya
Tamaso Maa Jyotir- Gamaya
Mrtyor-Maa Amrtam Gamaya
Om Saantih Saantih Shaantih."

(Brihadaranyaka Upanishads 1.3.28)

Introduction

Education is the key factor that transforms one's dream into reality through a life-long continuous process. Education develops 'making livelihood', makes more civilized and promotes rational thinking with civic senses. It is a precondition for uplifting individuals and society as the progress of education empowers nations, making them strong and prosperous. It helps one become cultured and equip oneself to cope with life's challenges. It becomes more effective in fulfilling present needs and restoring societal harmony. Education promotes economic growth, empowers quality citizens, develops moral and spiritual values and prepares one to fight against corruption. It enhances the dignity of human beings and develops self-respect and universal brotherhood. Kofi Annan states, "Education is a human right with immense power to transform. On its foundation rest the cornerstones of freedom, democracy and sustainable development" (Lahiri, 2016, p. 1). Nelson Mandela proclaimed, "Education is the most powerful weapon which you can use to change the world" (Lahiri, 2016, p. 1).

In the contemporary era, Prof. Avul Pakir Jainulabdeen Abdul Kalam's educational thought has played the role of a catalyst to restore equality in society, the dignity of the individual, to adopt modern science and technology as per the needs of the society with the ability of our own resources. Prof. Abdul Kalam's concept of education has emphasized character formation and drive against illiteracy, unemployment and social evils. Prof. Abdul Kalamas a teacher worked atthe Indian Institute of Management (Ahmedabad), Indian Institute Management (Indore), as a visiting Professor at the Indian Institute of Management (Shillong), a professor at Anna University (Chennai), Chancellor of JSS University (Mysore), and a visiting faculty member at the Indian Institute of Space Science and Technology (Thiruvananthapuram). He loved meeting with students to share his experiences. His educational thoughts are expressed in his speeches and writings. His strong desire to learn transformed him from 'a village boy' to a 'missile man', the people's president of India and a great teacher of the nation. According to Prof. Abdul Kalam, the three major visions of education are: 'Freedom' (freedom as we get an education), 'Development' (GDP as well as social and economic development) and 'Stand up' (strength and prosperity). He believes that education is a dynamic and innovative experience in life, and it continues up to the last breath.

The educational thoughts of Prof. Abdul Kalam can be explored in terms of the meaning of education, the aims and objectives of education, the curriculum of education, the role of the teacher, the method of teaching, the concept of the student, the concept of the teacher, student-teacher relations, the role of parents in education, value education, science education, teacher education, inclusive education and the concept autonomous learner in modern education.

Development of Indian Education System in Post-Independent Era

Education is the prime need of humankind; it generates not only knowledge but is also a key factor in the modification of behaviour, generating employment, reducing crime and making the nation's future. It depends on the curriculum of education, the goals of education, the role of the teacher, the method of teaching, and the role of parents and educational institutions. The Indian education system has evolved from the Rig-Vedic age to the contemporary era. The modern education system is the contributory form of Swami Dayananda Saraswati, Shree Aurobindo Ghosh, Rabindra Nath Tagore, Mohandas Karam Chand Gandhi, Jiddu Krishnamurthy, Dr Jakir Husain, Swami Vivekananda and so many eminent educationists and over and above Prof. Abdul Kalam. Prof. Abdul Kalam motivated children and youth to acquire knowledge and for nation-building through his motivational speech.

The UNO, in its Universal Declaration of Human Rights (UDHR) adopted by the United Nations General Assembly, in Paris, on 10th December 1948, stated in Article 26 that everyone has the right to education. It shall be free and compulsory in the elementary and fundamental stages. Education shall be directed to fulfil human personality, respect human rights, promote understanding, tolerance and friendship among nations, and restore peace.

In 1990, from the 5th to the 9th of March, UNESCO, UNDP, UNFPA, UNICEF, and the World Bank launched the first World Conference in Jomtien Thailand on 'basic learning needs'. During the meeting, 155 countries and 1500 delegates from government and non-government organisations adopted 'Education for All' (EFA). Article 1 of the conference stated that every person — child, youth and adult shall benefit from educational opportunities designed to meet their basic needs. From 26th to 28th April 2000, Dakar (Senegal) World Education Conference had taken a collective commitment to achieve the goal of EFA—gender equality in education by 2005 and to achieve UEE by 2015. But the goal was not fulfilled. The World Education Forum met in the Republic of Korea from 18th to

21st May 2015 and revised the deadline to 2030; the extended goal is 'Equitable and inclusive quality education in and lifelong learning for all by 2030'. It also focused on early child care and child with special needs (CWSN), promoting learning and life skills, quality education and gender equality.

Article 21A of the Indian Constitution Part-III states, "The State shall provide free and compulsory education to all children of 6 to 14 years in such manner as the State, may by law determine" (https://www.brainyias.com/article-21a-of-indian-constitution/). The 'Fundamental Rights of Citizens' includes the right to elementary education for the age group 6-14years and classes i-viii.

Article 45 of the Indian constitution Part-IV 'Directive Principles of State Policy' states that, "The state shall endeavour to provide within a period of ten years from the commencement of this Constitution, for free and compulsory education for all children until they complete the age of 14 years" (http://righttoeducation.in/how-was-original-article-45-constitution)

The University Education Commission (1948) suggested that Indian education must be rooted in its cultural heritage. According to the University Education Commission, "If we exclude spiritual training in our institutions, we would be untrue to our whole historical development." (Bandyopadhyay, 2019, p. 208). The commission emphasised the development of competent leaders for the nation, the development of agriculture, arts, medicine, science and technology with the development of high ideals of life such as justice, truthfulness, and righteousness, the right type of attitudes and values of life integrated with the way of life. According to the commission, the development of humanism, idealism, and tolerance is the vision of education. (The Report of Education Commission, December 1948-August 1949 Volume. 1, In Bandyopadhyay, 2019, p. 209).

The Secondary Education Commission (1952-53) emphasised value inculcation as well as character building as the goal of education and to develop quality citizens with strong national and social feeling and mentality to sacrifice for the nation, leadership quality, capacity to earn money and human Virtues. The commission recommended, "The supreme end of the educative process should be the training of the character and personality of students in such a way that they will be able to realise their full potentialities and contribute to the well-being of the community" (Report of the Secondary Education Commission In Bandyopadhyay, 2019, p. 214).

The Sri Prakash Committee on Religious and Moral Instruction (1959) recommended teaching moral and spiritual values in educational institutions, a comparative study of lives and teachings of great religious leaders, and a few minutes of silent meditation or prayer before the class works. At the elementary stage, apart from moral and spiritual education, "work is worship" should be developed among the students. At the higher class, comparative religion and history of religion should be given due importance as a study course (Bandyopadhyay, 2019, p. 216)

The Indian Education Commission (1964-66) emphasized that the school system's serious defect is the absence of provision for education in social, moral and spiritual values. The Commission recommended the universalisation of elementary education, vocationalisation of education and integration with work experience, and strengthening of science education and research (Bandyopadhyay, 2019, p. 219).

The National Policy on Education (1986) has emphasised the child's moral development with unity and integration. The recommendations are the universalisation of elementary education (UEE), vocationalisation of higher secondary education, operation blackboard, development of technical education and social relevance, education for girls, value-oriented education and national integration in education. (The

National Policy on Education 1986. In Bandyopadhyay, 2019, p. 220)

Delors Commission's Resolution in 1996 (https://en.wikipedia.org/wiki/Delors Report, para. 3) The Delors Commission accepted four pillars of education:

a. *Learning to know:* The term 'learning to know' refers to developing one's concentration, memory skills and thinking ability. Every individual has dormant potential. Learning manifests physical ability, aesthetic sense and aptitude to communicate.
b. *Learning to do:* The term 'learning to do' means the development of individual skills and their effective use in the global economy and society. It is associated with the issue of occupational training. Learning to do means acquiring occupational skills and the competence to deal with many situations and work in terms.
c. *Learning to be:* 'Learning to be' means learners should learn to become themselves. Education is meant for complete mind-body development, intelligence development, sensitivity, aesthetic appreciation and spirituality. Our education system has no proper mechanism to explore the potentialities of the human being. Present education has less emphasis on developing qualities like honesty, selflessness, fellow feelings, etc., which can be cultivated through value, morality and religious education.
d. *Learning to live together:* The term 'learning to live together' refers to unity and community feeling for society. It is related to the spirit of tolerance, the very nature of Indian culture. Violence threatens our present life, forming a depression in contrast with hope. Education should inculcate a spirit of empathy among students to develop a positive effect on their social behaviour throughout their lives by developing understanding with each other and resolving conflicts through dialogue and discussion.

The National Policy of Education 2020 has emphasised mandatory schooling for the age group of three to eighteen years (3-18) as twelve years of schooling. It promotes education through the mother tongue or regional language up to class five, educational monitoring through HECL under the Ministry of Education, vocational curriculum from class six, and freedom for students to choose the subject from any stream to fulfil the vision 'India a global knowledge supreme power'.

In the present society, with the development of scientific cum technological civilisation, man has secured material gains but is deprived of his/her inner peace and moral and spiritual values. Education is the potential tool to restructure society devoid of mental despair and value crisis. So education must address the issue of character formation along with the development of individual potentialities. Prof. Abdul Kalam's inspiring and motivating words always work as a catalyst for teachers and students, but his thoughts and contribution to the field of education are still unexplored.

Modern education is confronted with many legitimate questions, such as the definition, goal of education, the role of environments in education, teaching method, and medium of teaching and nature of science education. All these problems need a sound philosophical analysis. Prof. Abdul Kalam considers the present education defective in respect of educational goals, lack of proper guidance and inspiration, and the role of the teacher. These are the prominent cause of illiteracy, ignorance, unemployment, indiscipline and social evils. Prof. Abdul Kalam's educational philosophy greatly impacts students' motivation, creativity and science education; the role of parents, teachers and students' relationship for the perfection of learners leads to livelihood and national development.

It is seen that with the development of science and technology, our nation is going ahead, but corruption, crime, lawlessness, and violence are gradually increasing. Our daily newspapers and other media reveal that value crises and corruption have spread in every sphere of life. The atmosphere of schools and colleges is deteriorating. Students are in unhealthy competition among classmates, and they want to excel one another. Anxiety and fear lead one to be a psycho-patient. It sometimes leads to rivalries, jealousy and hatred among classmates. Sometimes malpractices in exam centers are the headline of leading newspapers. Teachers are being assaulted by their own students. Parents are neglected and tortured by their children. All these are glaring examples of the decline of values in our society. Moral and spiritual developments are the way to promote sympathy, tolerance, good feeling etc., to promote a favourable atmosphere. In this context, such type of education is needed to impart our country's moral values and heritage to promote sympathy, tolerance, good feelings and ideal character in life.

Prof. Abdul Kalam's 'Educational Philosophy' addresses the meaning of education, aims and objectives of education, curriculum of study, concept of teacher and teaching, concept of students, teacher, parents, moral values, women's education, spiritual education and youth education and science education as a modest step to meet all these problems.

Summary

Education is the precondition for the social, economic, political, moral, cultural and spiritual development of an individual as well as the nation. The UN declared education as a human right in 1948. Prof. Abdul Kalam enriched the Indian education system with the changes and needs of society and correlated the past and present in education. Studying the educational philosophy of Prof. Abdul Kalam is significant in respect of EFA –'Education For All'—a movement by UNESCO, the four pillars of education–resolution by the Delors Commission in 1996, recommendations of the University Education Commission– 1948, Secondary Education Commission– 1952-1953, Kothari Commission-1964-1966, National Education Policy–1986, National Education Policy 2020. Prof. Abdul Kalam's educational thought is a clear and distinct conception of the 20th century as well as the 21st century in an explanation of student-teacher relations, value-oriented, student and society-centric, job-oriented education and a clear directive to youth for the nation.

3
Educational Philosophy of Kalam

The educational Philosophy of Prof. Abdul Kalam is the coherence of Idealism, Naturalism, Realism, Humanism and Pragmatism.

Optimism

Prof. Abdul Kalam was an optimist by nature, and he encouraged promoting performance in life. He had a character of praising someone openly and criticizing privately. He loved his colleagues, even those who discouraged and hurt him badly. He was a little bit disappointed with the postponement of the parliamentary session. He alleged that the traceability of certain legislative seats degrades the democratic system. He treated the workouts of parliamentarians as a negative effect and a waste of the economy. According to Prof. Abdul Kalam, freedom means to make India free from poverty, illiteracy and unemployment and to make a peaceful India. He said freedom should be exercised to get rid of slavery. Hard work and strong determination are the best ways to free India from poverty, illiteracy and unemployment. He said if we do not work hard, we will surrender our fate to others. But Prof. Abdul Kalam believed that 'you can' India can' get rid of all these problems. Prof. Abdul Kalam, from his childhood, observed the seagulls flying on the seashore, making him realize that he wanted to be an aeronautical engineer. Prof. Abdul Kalam (1999) said, "Simple, provincial boy though I was, I was convinced that one day I, too, would soar up into the skies; indeed, I was the first child from Rameshwaram to fly." (Kalam & Tiwari, 1999, p. 13). He was visionary and planned for India Mission 2020. His vision was to consume collective energy for a broader purpose and greater benefit.

Nationalism

Prof. Abdul Kalam was a simple human being with a motto to serve the nation with all his potential and hard work. He believed that "the nation is bigger than any individual" and concentrated on developing our country's competencies. Prof. Abdul Kalam was delighted with the successful SLV-III (1980) launch of the Agni missile in 1989 by DRDO and the Pokhran Nuclear power test in 1998. The development of the Kalam-Raju stent, Kalam-Raju tablet (PC) and the formation of PURA are the key points of his reflection on Nationalism. According to Prof. Abdul Kalam, the motto of education is to inculcate "We can do it" among students to make them adequately efficient and to cope with the problems in life. Minimising cultural logs and making them creative, imaginative and innovative are the aspects of the nationalistic attitude of Prof. Abdul Kalam.

Patriotism

Prof. Abdul Kalam was very proud of his nation. He concentrated on the success of the SLV Project, despite the pain of the death of his father, mother and cousin. Prof. Abdul Kalam launched SLV-3 on 18th July 1980 from the SHAR Rocket launching station, and India was empowered as the fifth country for satellite launch compatibility. Prof. Abdul Kalam's experience from ISRO helped him utilize combined efforts in DRDL for the success of IGMDP. His dream project "Agni" missile was launched on 22nd May 1989. He said, "It is fire, in the heart of an Indian ... as it clings to the burning pride of this nation." (Kalam & Tiwari, 1999,

p. 15). In this regard, former President R. Venkataraman said that it was a tribute to the dedication, hard work and talent of Prof. Abdul Kalam. It has shown that Indians can develop and use advanced technology to tackle real-life problems. Prof. Abdul Kalam said, "Be active! Take on responsibility! Work for the things you believe in." (Kalam & Twari, 1999, p. 77). Dr Abdul Kalam emphasised creating enlightened citizens through equal opportunity for everyone and using it in a better way. Prof. Abdul Kalam suggested that the parliamentarians concentrate on developing five key areas: agriculture, education health care, infrastructure, information and communication technology and critical technology. He used to organize virtual conferences, virtual meetings and brainstorming sessions with experts in Rashtrapati Bhavan and cleared his files within five hours through a digital filing system.

Idealism

According to Prof. Abdul Kalam, education should be imparted based on spiritual values to develop enlightened citizens. Education aims to realize the ultimate truth and prepare for a holy life. Prof. Abdul Kalam said, "... one's communion with an eternal source of hidden knowledge within oneself — which each individual is bidden to seek and find for himself or herself." (Kalam & Tiwari, 1999, Prelude. x). Prof. Abdul Kalam also said, "We are all born with a divine fire in us. Our efforts should be to give wings to this fire and fill the world with the glow of its goodness." (Kalam & Tiwari, 1999, Prelude. xvi). Prof. Abdul Kalam believed, "I had been taught that true reality lay beyond the material world in the spiritual realm. And that knowledge could be obtained only through inner experience." (Kalam & Tiwari, 1999, Prelude. x). In this context it would not be irrelevant to point out an incident involving President Prof. Kalam. The fact was: on the 15th August 2003, the President of India Dr Kalam was hosting a reception for more than two to three thousand guests at 5:30 p.m. But from the early morning the weather was so cloudy and portending heavier showers. Prof. Kalam's secretary P. M. Nair was very anxious about the situation, but Prof. Kalam was so cool and said to Mr. Nair at about 12:38 p.m. 'Don't worry'. He pointed a hand skywards and continued, I have spoken there. By 2 p.m. the rain had stopped and the reception in the lawns was smoothly conducted (Nair, pp. 28-29). He loved art and music as part of the preparation for an idealistic approach. The terms 'divine fire in us', 'faith in God', 'reality lay beyond the material' and 'inner experience' refers to Prof. Abdul Kalam's Idealistic Approach.

Realism

Realism emphasizes useful and purposeful education for individual and social development with the use of material resources to solve real-life problems. Prof. A. P. J. Abdul Kalam has emphasized the development of the spirit of inquiry, creativity and innovation, the capacity to use high-end technology and entrepreneurial and moral leadership qualities. Parents and teachers must be the real-life heroes of the student community. So, education is to cope with the practical problems of life. In this regard, he develops the concept of PURA. He also believed that education is the preparation for life by developing physical and mental capacities, training of senses, and adjustment to the environment. This is a realistic attitude of Prof. Abdul Kalam.

Naturalism

Prof. Abdul Kalam advocated for complete freedom for children in learning and development. He believed that the child is the centre point of education, emphasized the child's interests and tendencies, and stressed drawing out creative and innovative ideas. Therefore, he can be considered a naturalist.

Pragmatism

According to Prof. Abdul Kalam, the motto of education is to inculcate the concept of "I can do it" and "We can do it" instead of "I can not do it" or "We can not do it' among students. Also, the concept of 'what can I do for you' in place of 'what can you do for me', and to make them able to cope with the practical problems in life by minimising cultural log and to make them creative, imaginative and innovative in practical life by the development of confidence, self-respect, dignity and to prepare them to transform their dreams into reality.

Humanism

Man is at the centre point of Prof. Abdul Kalam's educational philosophy. He concentrated on the welfare of men, particularly people of rural areas or unprivileged sectors, to develop and restore peace on earth and equality in education. Prof. Abdul Kalam said, "What they dream of can become possible, that they can have anything that comprises a good life: health, education, the freedom to pursue their goals, and above all, peace" (Kalam, 2002, Prelude. xi). All these are signs of his Humanistic Approach. It is true that, nothing was unimportant to Dr Kalam. All the letters and e-mails addressed to Rashtapati Bhavan has been given same priority to attend and answer in morning meetings (Nair, 2011, p. 41).

4
Meaning of Education

Introduction

Education is the most powerful accelerator for the growth and prosperity of a nation. The present education system of all nations is based on needs and ideologies of their own. According to Prof. A. P. J. Abdul Kalam, transforming India into a developed nation by 2020 is the prime motto of Indian education. He believes that the people of India must acquire employability skills and job-oriented education with competency around the globe. He was more interested in widespread education awareness, particularly in rural areas and among the urban poor underprivileged. Prof. Abdul Kalam's educational philosophy is reflected in his books, autobiography, lectures and speeches, articles, and poems. It is understood through the Conceptual and Relational Content analysis and Exploratory, Exegetical, Thought experiments and Critical Philosophical methods.

Meaning of Education

According to Prof. Abdul Kalam, education is about inculcating the spirit of "I can do it' and "we can do it". The word 'inculcate' is derived from the Latinword 'inculcare'. It means the process through which something is being stamped into someone's brain. Prof. Abdul Kalam clearly stated that education is the process of inculcating among students the concept of 'I can do it' in place of 'I can not do it' and 'we can do it' in place of 'we can not do it' and the concept of 'what can I do for you' in place of 'what can you do for me'. So, education is an active process. He believed that it is the process of drawing out and developing the inherent dormant quality of students. Here the term 'Drawing out' refers to searching out the quality of students. 'Developing' means growing or evolving inherent dormant quality. According to Prof. Abdul Kalam, knowledge has three major components—creativity, righteousness and courage. Prof. Abdul Kalam defined the term 'creativity' by saying that learning gives creativity, creativity leads him to think, thinking provides knowledge, and knowledge makes that person great. Creativity is expressed through the manifestation of hidden potentiality with self-confidence and self-reliance. Thus, education promotes creativity.

Prof. Abdul Kalam defined the term 'righteousness' in this way: righteousness in the heart brings beauty in character, beauty in character brings harmony at home, harmony at home brings order in the nation, and order in the nation brings peace in the world.

Prof. Abdul Kalam defined courage in this way: courage leads one to think differently, to invent an unexplored path, to discover the impossible, to combat life's problems and finally to achieve success in missions. All these make one become an enlightened person. In this context, Prof. Abdul Kalam said that education is an endless journey through knowledge and enlightenment. Here, 'Knowledge' means 'to know', 'to do', 'to be' and 'to live together'. According to Prof. Abdul Kalam, education is a lifelong journey to be an enlightened citizen. 'Enlighten' means the manifestation of innate dormant potentiality, i.e., the divinity in man (the permanent truth), as well as the manifestation of physical, social and emotional development with the feeling of nationalism and leadership quality and to restore harmony in family and society as well as corruption free and better to live in.

Prof. Abdul Kalam, in his autobiography, defined education as "... one's communion with an eternal source of hidden knowledge within oneself — which each individual is bidden to seek and find for himself or herself." (Kalam & Tiwari, 1999, Prelude p. x). According to Swami Vivekananda, we are divine in nature, "Amritasya Putra", and Prof. Abdul Kalam said, "We are all born with a divine fire in us. Our efforts should be to give wings to this fire and fill the world with the glow of its goodness." (Kalam & Tiwari, 1999, Prelude p. xvi). So divinity is our innate nature. Prof. Abdul Kalam believed that he who knows others is learned, but the wise person is one who knows himself. It is stated that learning without wisdom is of no use; it is pertinent to point out Prof. Abdul Kalam's view "I had been taught that true reality lay beyond the material world in the spiritual realm. And that knowledge could be obtained only through inner experience." (Kalam & Tiwari, 1999, p. 19) So the true reality – the spiritual realm could be obtained only through inner experiences. He said knowledge lies dormant within us and is not yet manifested. Every person has the tendency to manifest it, i.e., the oneness with other people and to know the reality beyond the material world. Knowledge does not come from outside; it comes from within. This is an Idealistic approach.

It is pertinent to point out a practical story of Prof. Abdul Kalam to understand his concept of education. Prof. Abdul Kalam, a student of Aeronautics at MIT with his six teammates, was assigned a project, and Abdul Kalam was assigned to complete a drawing design for the aerodynamics of a low-level attack aircraft by Prof. Srinivasan, director of MIT. They were working for a few weeks. One day, Prof. Srinivasan in a surprise visit, asked Abdul Kalam about the assignment and being disappointed with his performance, Dr Srinivasan said to Abdul Kalam, "This is just not good enough, Kalam." I expected much better from you. Abdul Kalam was ashamed of this, and it made him determined to prove himself. By Sunday evening Abdul Kalam hadalmost completed the assignment. Prof. Srinivasan came to check the progress of work and was surprised by his work. Prof. Abdul Kalam said, "After examining my work, Prof. Srinivasan hugged me affectionately and patted my back in appreciation. He said, "I knew I was putting you under stress and asking you to meet an impossible deadline. I never expected you to perform so well." (Kalam & Tiwari, 1999, p. 20) It can be concluded that education is the process of overcoming failure and achieving success or preparing a person to cope with problems in life. In this context Prof. Abdul Kalam defined F. A. I. L. as the first attempt at learning. In 1979, SLV-III – the dream project of Prof. Kalam was dropped in the Bay of Bengal, but in July 1980, he achieved the desired success. So, learning comes from failure. Education is an endless journey through knowledge and enlightenment, and education is the process of overcoming failure. It is a realistic approach.

So, according to Prof. Abdul Kalam, education is to culminate professional capability, build confidence and will power to know, to do, to be and to live together by bravely combating problems of life and nation. (Kalam, 2003. p. 5). So, the educational Philosophy of Prof. Abdul Kalam is the coherent blend of Idealism, Realism, Pragmatism, Naturalism and Humanism.

5
Aims and Objectives of Education

The aims and objectives of the education of Prof. Abdul Kalam are analysed from his writings and speeches using Relational content analysis, Prescriptive and Exegetical Philosophical methods. Prof. Abdul Kalam wanted to focus on five components in education: research and inquiry, creativity and innovation, the capacity to use high-end technology, entrepreneurship and moral leadership quality.

To Develop Research and Inquiry

According to Prof. Abdul Kalam, for the nation's sustainable development, we should adopt an organizational policy of promoting scientific temper among students through the openness of communication, exchange of learning materials, the collaboration of universities, participation of worldwide seminars etc. So the aim of education is to develop the capacity for research and inquiry among students.

To Develop Creativity and Innovation

According to Prof. Abdul Kalam, the primary goal of education is to develop inquiry, innovativeness, creativity, technological development, and entrepreneurship to become self-directed and self-dependent. A mindset to respect authority and properly question authority is also the vision of education. So the development of creativity, a sense of dignity, self-respect, self-reliance and innovation is the goal of education.

To Enhance the Capacity to Use Technology

Enhancing the capacity to use technology and energy is the need of the present situation. Education must have the vision to develop the capacity to know how to use modern technology and to become energy dependent nation for the vision of 2020. So education has to prepare students to develop and use technology to meet the challenges in life.

To Develop Vocational Efficiency and Entrepreneurship

According to Prof. Abdul Kalam, education must lay emphasis on employment generation to become a self-reliant and economically developed person as well as a nation. It requires vocational training from school life to higher education to develop creativity and ignite them. Creativity comes through creative learning habits. The child must dream of becoming a doctor, engineer, scientist, teacher, political leader, diplomat or astronaut, and education must add wings to fulfill the dream. So the aim of education is to make one fly in dreams, commitment to fulfilling dreams and skill development to fulfill the dream. Prof. Abdul Kalam pointed out, "When the student passes out of senior secondary schools, they should have two certificates of passing 10+2 examinations and of a specific skill he acquired. It will help them to get a job and to be aware of the social needs and nature of industries and productions of that time being." (*India Today*, 2015 July 28th Kalam's expectations from the Indian education system).

To Develop Enlightened Citizens with Leadership Quality

According to Prof. Abdul Kalam, the prime motto of education is to promote democratic values among children and help them become enlightened citizens. This contributes to removing social evils, fostering economic development overcoming unemployment, eliminating poverty and terrorism, and fostering peaceful competition for a happy, strong and prosperous nation. Children are the future citizens of the country, and they have to shoulder the nation's responsibilities. The strength of a nation depends on the strength, will, courage, clarity of thinking and the power of decision-making and leadership quality. So education should instill in children leadership qualities with creativity and innovation. Prof. Abdul Kalam emphasized that creative leadership should be combined with entrepreneurship to address unemployment.

The aim of education is to transform children into leaders of the country. According to Prof. Abdul Kalam, a child asks, "What can you do for me?" and education turns it into "What can I do for you?" So the transformation is from "What can you do for me? to "What can I do for you?"

To Retain the Smile on the Face of Our Children

Prof. Abdul Kalam said, "Your children are not your children. They are the sons and daughters of Life's longing for itself. They come through you but not from you. You may give them your love but not your thoughts. For they have their own thoughts" (Kalam & Tiwari, 1999, p. 10). Prof. Abdul Kalam suggested that children are the greatest wealth of the nation. They are like blossoms, happy and fresh. Prof. Abdul Kalam appealed to parents and teachers not to burden them with their frustrations and hopelessness and not to pollute their pure minds. According to Prof. Abdul Kalam, small children always smile, but their smile gradually reduces when they carry a big bag to primary school. In the secondary section, the smile further reduces, and in higher secondary, it virtually vanishes. It is essential to ensure that the education system must have the vision to retain the smiles on the faces of children by reducing the theoretical burden from the primary level to the higher level of education. Therefore, education can be transmitted in a joyful environment.

To Develop Scientific Attitude based on Spirituality

Prof. Abdul Kalam, with the influence of Swami Vivekananda, said that concentration of mind is the way to acquire knowledge. The strength and force of the glow come through concentration of the mind. Prof. Abdul Kalam wanted to develop a creative mind among children and motivate them to discover the world's secrets, i.e. spirituality. Concentration of the mind is the way to build self-dignity, self-respect and self-reliance. He believed that questioning is the source of science education as well as knowing the hidden potentiality of man, i.e. divinity. So, the aims and objectives of education are to develop a scientific attitude with a spiritual foundation.

To Develop Character with Human Values

Moral leadership is the presupposition of human development. Education must focus on developing the feeling of universal brotherhood and affinity. Social justice is the key to the success of democracy because we are equal before the eyes of the law. Prof. Abdul Kalam advocated for the courage to fight against injustice to restore equal opportunities, dignity, self-respect, and character building. He has emphasized individuality, independent identity and individual difference and over and above humanity in the heart like honesty, courage and righteousness as part of the character.

To Develop the Concept of Living Together

According to Prof. Abdul Kalam, children should learn to live together and die for the nation. So to develop a sense of service and sacrifice with moral and spiritual values to build up the nation with economic prosperity and peace are the vision of education. Families and parents are responsible for instilling righteousness in the hearts of children and fostering a sense of unity towards the nation.

To Develop Nationalism with Universal Brotherhood

At present, all the nations of the world are mutually interdependent. Education must have the vision to develop the mentality of interdependence, a feeling of universal brotherhood, and fellow feelings. So, education opens the avenues to explain the national problem with an international look. Responsibility, sympathy, fellow feeling, and cooperation help to correlate nationalism with internationalism. Prof. Abdul Kalam has emphasized global fellow-feeling through education in its true meaning.

So, the aims and objectives of education are skill development and entrepreneurship, a sense of dignity and self-respect, scientific attitude, character building, retaining smiles on the face of children, enlightened citizen with leadership qualities and transformation of "what can you do for me?" to "what can I do for you?"

6

Curriculum of Study

Prof. Abdul Kalam believed in the development of agriculture, education, health care, information and communication technology and infrastructure in an integrated manner with value-oriented education to build up leadership qualities to lead the nation with the capacity for decision-making, envisioning, planning, and managing failures.

The educational philosophy of Prof. Abdul Kalam is reflected in his writings and speeches, and it can be understood through relational content analysis, diagnostic and critical philosophical methods of analysis.

Prof. Abdul Kalam strongly believed that the future of India depends on children because the nation's strength is millions of youths. These youths can be transformed into valuable human resources through the educational process. So, the curriculum must be connected with the societal, occupational and technological needs with high moral values of life to make the world better to live in. The curriculum should be based on science and technology to generate creativity and innovativeness by providing learning by doing and training skills from the primary level to higher education. Prof. Abdul Kalam as an idealist, emphasized art, music, literature, education and spiritual education; in a word, in curriculum, brain and heart must be given equal importance.

Prof. Abdul Kalam believed that the education system should maintain high educational standards to compete with international institutions. So, education, particularly higher education, must be empowered by government and private funds to promote research and higher education, and incentives must be provided for teachers and students. So world-class salary structures, collaboration with international projects, research on national challenges and research on agriculture and industries are to be given top priority. For healthcare hospitals with PHSC-Private healthcare centers, applying tale-medication technology in healthcare service requires higher quality medical laboratories and qualified faculty for health and hospital services. Skill development training must be provided for youth in a two-month summer internship programme, particularly on sanitation, water purification and maintenance of village ponds. Prof. Abdul Kalam believed that the education of girls should be given top priority. So, with the help of MPs and MLAs, funding toilet for girls, drinking water, electricity, and child-friendly infrastructure can be improved. Prof. Abdul Kalam wanted to set up a different societal grid, like a knowledge grid to provide knowledge, a health grid to provide health care, and an e-governance-grid for transparency in government service. The formation of PURA (Providing Urban Amenities to Rural Areas) is essential for the holistic development of people and the nation to be morally upright, intellectually superior, and to lead an enriched quality of life.

In addressing Delhi school principals and teachers, Prof. Abdul Kalam suggested providing their children 1-2 periods of skill development training in the nearest ITI colleges or private workshops. He also suggested setting up a mobile laboratory for 12 classes so that students could learn, particularly ICT and chemical laboratory ('Giving Light' Vol. 7, July 2015). Regarding peace and prosperity, Prof. Abdul Kalam suggested restoring democratic values and not developing cross-border terrorism and naxalism. Prof. Abdul Kalam was hopeful that by 2020, there would be zero poverty, 100% literacy, quality health care, value-added quality education, and job-oriented professional skill development. Prof. Abdul Kalam is hopeful that "If we channelize our integrated efforts towards the development of India before 2020, then the growth of the nation is certain." According to Prof. Abdul Kalam, the vision of education is – to reduce rural and urban division, social and urban discrimination, corruption and crime-free responsive governance, development of agriculture, industries, technology and job-oriented and sustainable growth of the nation through education.

Prof. Abdul Kalam pointed out the different stages of education — primary, secondary, and higher education. He defined the curriculum of education in this way.

According to Prof. Abdul Kalam, "When students pass out of senior secondary schools, they should have two certificates of passing 10+2 examination and of a specific skill acquired by him during schooling". (*India Today*, 2015 July 28th, Kalam's expectations from the Indian education system). Therefore, in addition to the regular curriculum, students should receive special training for skill development and entrepreneurship. Dr Abdul Kalam defined education as the primary driving force of personal growth, so it requires skill-based education at the school level. So, curriculum must be designed to produce many employment generators, not just employment seekers.

Prof. Abdul Kalam said, "I studied up to the tenth standard through the vernacular medium and later picked up English." He advised that teachers should teach children science in their mother tongue" (*The Hindu*, 2011, January 20th, He is in favour of imparting science education in the mother tongue, Para. 2). So, he was in favour of imparting science education through the mother tongue at an early stage.

Spiritual education, like the preaching of saints and religious books to acquire educational values, faith in God and spiritual harmony are the important aspects of the curriculum.

The curriculum should focus on science and technology including nano-sciences, biotechnology, IT, industries, entrepreneurship, management skills and academic subjects. Educational institutions should facilitate entrepreneurship, the lesson of truth, the path of righteousness, service for the masses, and faith in God in the curriculum.

Prof. Abdul Kalam was deeply concerned about the advancement of technology. He suggested that Indian youth should not be without ethics, a world-class higher education or world-class skill. So, the provision for experiential learning and learning by doing should be included with the academic subjects to develop values, humanity, discipline, coordination, non-violence, entrepreneurship and management skills.

The curriculum of the study includes academic subjects along with entrepreneurship. The educational curriculum covers Nano-sciences, biotechnology, IT, industries, entrepreneurship, management skills and academic subjects like language, sciences, humanities, and commerce, with life history, ethics, value education, games and sports and preaches of saints. So, the curriculum of the study encompasses academic subjects and entrepreneurship.

7
Concept and Qualities of a Teacher

Prof. Abdul Kalam's concept of a teacher and the qualities of a teacher are derived from his writings, speeches and incidents of his life through content analysis, conceptual analysis as well as Philosophical methods such as the thought experiment method and exegetical analysis.

Concept of a Teacher

Prof. Abdul Kalam believed that great schools must have smart classrooms, quality teachers with righteousness, and professionally sound and morally upright happy youth. "The teacher, the child's window to learning and knowledge, has to play the role model in generating creativity in the child." (Kalam, 2002, p. 23). The teacher must be a role model for students and be able to generate creativity among children. Dr Abdul Kalam believed that teaching is a noble profession that shapes the child's character, calibre, and future. He wanted to be remembered after his demise as a good teacher as the highest honour to him.

Prof. Abdul Kalam said that if you give him a child to nurture for seven years, then afterwards, neither God or nor the devil can change that child. So, the teacher, the Guru, has a great role in shaping students' dreams to build up the next generation. A teacher should be innovative and stimulative. They should improve their knowledge and qualifications and help students develop broad thinking.

Prof. Abdul Kalam recognized that Shri Subramania Iyer was a great teacher at his school. Shri Subramania Iyer used to teach theoretical knowledge with practical examples. Therefore, a teacher must teach theoretical knowledge with practical examples. Teachers not only teach but also shape student's lives to help them achieve their aims and fulfill their dreams. Prof. Abdul Kalam's teacher Iyadurai Solomon told him, "To succeed in life and achieve results, you must understand and master three mighty forces — desire, belief, and expectation." (Kalam & Tiwari, 1999, p. 12). Prof. Kalam said, "My teacher, Iyadurai Solomon, was an ideal guide for young minds. His warm and open-minded attitude made his students feel very comfortable in class. He used to say that a good student could learn more from a bad teacher than a poor student from even a skilled teacher." (Kalam & Tiwari, 1999, p. 12) So it entails that teachers must have a warm and open-minded attitude toward their students. Prof. Abdul Kalam recognized his debt to Dr Vikram Sarabhai, Dr Satish Dhawan and Dr Brahm Prakash and said, "I certainly owe a great debt of knowledge and inspiration to the distinguished lineage of Indian scientists that included Vikram Sarabhai, Satish Dhawan and Brahm Prakash." (Kalam & Tiwari, 1999, Prelude p. xiv)

Prof. Abdul Kalam learned a lot from Dr Vikram Sarabhai. He said about Dr Sarabhai, "He never gave directions; rather, through a free exchange of views, he led us forward into new terrain which often revealed an unforeseen solution" (Kalam & Tiwari, 1999, p. 44). Prof. Abdul Kalam said, "The credit for the successful SLV-3 flight goes, first, to the giants of the Indian space programme, Prof. Sarabhai in particular, who had preceded this effort." (Kalam & Tiwari, 1999, p. 100). Dr Sarabhai consoled Prof. Abdul Kalam after his father's death and said, "When troubles come, try to understand the relevance of your sufferings. Adversity always presents opportunities for introspection." (Kalam & Tiwari, 1999, p. 5). So, the teacher must have faith that errors are an opportunities to promote innovation and develop new ideas.

Prof. Abdul Kalam was inspired by his teacher Dr Satish Dhawan of the Indian Institute of Science. Dr Dhawan taught him to prepare meticulous planning. Prof. Abdul Kalam learned from Satish Dhawan that education should culminate in professional capability that develops confidence and willpower to combat many problems in order to achieve goals bravely. Dr Satish Dhawan consoled Prof. Abdul Kalam after the death of his brother-in-law Jalaluddin. Prof. Abdul Kalam said Dr Satish Dhawan took responsibility for the failure of SLV-III in 1979 and met the press and said, "Today we failed, but our team has superb qualities; we will succeed next time". So, a teacher must have the capacity to develop a student's professional capability, confidence and willpower. Prof. Abdul Kalam humbly recognized and thankful to his professors Sponder, Prof. K.A.V. Padalai and Prof. Narasingha Rao of Madras Institute of Technology (MIT), who helped him fulfill his intellectual hunger as well as to be a renowned scientist. So, a teacher must have the capacity to fulfill the intellectual hunger of a student.

Dr Brahma Prakash inspired Prof. Abdul Kalamand Prof. Kalam said, "Dr Brahm Prakash was a very wise counselor who gave me valuable guidance whenever I deviated from my mission objectives." (Kalam & Tiwari, 1999, p. 97) Dr Brahma was a wise counselor and played an important role in shaping Prof. Abdul Kalam's leadership skills. The sense of humility of Dr Brahma Prakash helped Prof. Abdul Kalam to discard his aggressive approach. So, the teacher must be a wise counselor and a valuable guide to developing the leadership qualities of students.

According to Prof. Abdul Kalam a teacher is like a 'ladder' to climb up in life. The moto of the teacher is to ignite the minds of children. He said, "...the teacher should not spread the poison of social inequality and communal intolerance in the minds of innocent children". (Kalam & Tiwari, 1999, p. 9). In response to a question, Prof. Abdul Kalam asked "First, you tell me what you would like to be remembered for? President, scientist, writer, missile man, India 2020, Target 3 billion ...what? Prof. Abdul Kalam replied, "Teacher." He also said, "One is blessed if one can die working, standing tall without any long-drawn ailing. Goodbyes should be short, really short." In his final moments, he was standing, working and lecturing; he accumulated nothing other than love and good wishes of the people. The man is gone, but the mission lives on.(Srijan Pal Singh, Facebook post, Rupanwair p. 228).

Qualities of a Teacher

Passion for teaching, allowing thinking, putting the student ahead, creating pressure to explore and being free from a communal mentality are the qualities of a teacher.

1. Passion for Teaching

According to Prof. Abdul Kalam, "Bread baked without love is a bitter bread that feeds but half a man's hunger" — those who cannot work with their hearts achieve but a hollow, half-hearted success that breeds bitterness all around." (Kalam & Tiwari, 1999, p. 45) Prof. Abdul Kalam, in his childhood, when he was reading in a Panchayat primary school of Rameswaram, his teacher Mathu Iyer was too interested in him because the child Kalam performed very well in-class exercises. The teacher Mathu Iyer met with the father of Prof. Abdul Kalam and praised child Kalam as a very good student. One day, Prof. Abdul Kalam was absent from his school and on the same evening, his teacher Mathu Iyer came to his house to ask his father about his absence from school and whether he could do anything for him. Prof. Abdul Kalam'shand writing was very poor, and his teacher Mathu Iyer advised him to improve his handwriting. The teacher Mathu Iyer loved teaching and took a personal interest in pupils. The teacher, Mathu Iyer, not only influenced pupils but also shaped them with good habits. So the teacher must have a passion for teaching.

2. Allowing Thinking

One day Prof. Abdul Kalam's teacher Sri Siva Subramania Iyer was teaching about birds' flight depicting the wings, tail and body structure with head position. He explained how they change their direction while flying and change the shape of the body with it. At the end of the discussion, the teacher Siva Subramania Iyer asked them whether they understood. Along with other classmates, young Kalam politely answered that he did not understand. On that evening, all students of the class were accompanied by the teacher Siva Subramania Iyer to the sea of Rameswaram. He showed how sea birds were flying with a secret chirping voice. The teacher explained the tail position, flapping wings and twisting the tail when birds fly. Prof. Abdul Kalam asked his teacher, "Where is the engine, and how is it powered?" The teacher explained that the bird is powered by its own life and motivation. All the students and Prof. Abdul Kalam understood the bird's flying dynamics theory with practical examples. Prof. Abdul Kalam said this experience made him think and decide on his future course of study as flight science. He asked his teacher, "Sir, please tell me how to progress further in learning all about flight?" His teacher patiently answered him to complete the eighth-grade and high school exams and then go to college to study flight sciences. In 1954, Prof. Abdul Kalam was admitted to MIT for aeronautical engineering. According to Prof. Abdul Kalam, asking his teacher the question and getting a satisfying answer from the teacher Shri Siva Subramania Iyer, ignited him. So, the teacher must have the quality of igniting youth and creating an atmosphere by allowing them to think, ask questions and get satisfactory answers.

3. Putting the Students Ahead

According to Prof. Abdul Kalam, in a photo session, his teacher, Prof. Sponder invited him and said, "Come and sit with me in the front." He said the speech of his professor inspired him - "You are my best student, and hard work will help you bring a great name for your teachers in the future." (Kalam & Tiwari, 1999, p. 21) Prof. Abdul Kalam said he had an opportunity at St. Joseph's College to witness his Mathematics teacher Prof. Thothari Iyengar. Prof. Thothari Iyengar used to teach Modern algebra, statistics and complex variables. Prof. Abdul Kalam recalled in the year 1952, Professor Thothari Iyengar delivered a lecture on ancient Mathematics and Astronomy of India and introduced mathematicians and astronomers of India, namely Aryabhatta, Srinivasa, Ramanujam, Brahmagupta, and Bhakaracharya. He said that Aryabhatta was born in 476 A.D. in Kusuna-Puna (presently Patna) and discovered the value of pie and earth takes about 365 days to orbit around the sun. Professor Thothari puts the students ahead in developing insight and creativity among them. So, the teacher must improve the will power of students to actualize their dream and put them ahead.

4. Creating Pressure to Explore Capabilities

During the third year of his studies, Prof. Abdul Kalam at MIT, Chennai, was assigned a project to design a low-level attack aircraft with his six other classmates. Prof. Abdul Kalam's responsibility was to complete the aerodynamic and structural design of the project under the supervision of Professor Srinivasan, Director of MIT. When Professor Srinivasan reviewed the progress of the project, he was disappointed with the progress of Prof. Abdul Kalam and said, "Look, young man, today is Friday afternoon. I give you three days. If by Monday morning I don't get the configuration design your scholarship will be stopped." (Kalam & Tiwari, 1999, p. 20)

Without a scholarship, Prof. Abdul Kalam could not continue his studies. Prof. Abdul Kalam, along with his teammates, started working together around the clock. On Sunday, Prof. Srinivasan suddenly came to supervise the project and said with appreciation, "I knew I was putting you under stress and asking you to meet a difficult deadline; you have done a great job in system design." (Kalam & Tiwari, 1999, p. 20)

5. To be a Role Model

According to Prof. Abdul Kalam, "When you are growing up, say till the age of fifteen, the best role model I can think of would be your father, your mother and your school teachers." (Kalam & Tiwari, 1999, p. 22) According to him, no other profession in the world is more important to society than a teacher. Teachers are the backbone of any country, the pillar upon which aspirations are converted into realities. The teacher's responsibilities are to nurture his own life as a noble person that the students can follow. Teachers are students' best friends, and he knows to excel with his students. They must create an atmosphere among students so that they can understand the lesson for life-long. (Chauhan, 2017, A Study of Thinking on Education System of Prof. Abdul Kalam, Vol. 5, Issue 8, p. 17-22) A student up to 10+2 class spent approximately 25000 hours in school, so the school environment and teacher's behaviour played an important role in the student's future. So, the teacher plays the role of Guru to build up the moral character of students and to make them able to use technology. Students see dreams, and teachers make them confident to fulfill them. Creativity is the key to the success of the future, and it develops at the primary level of education. The teacher is responsible for shaping a student's character, creativity development and interest in learning. Any deviation among students in academic performance noticed by the teachers should be brought to the parents. (Kalam, 2003, Teachers should be role models). In 1958 Prof. Abdul Kalam joined the DRDO Aeronautical Development Establishment at Bangalore. He took charge of the development of hovercraft, which required the development of a ducted contra-rotating propeller. Prof. Abdul Kalam did not know how to design a contra-rotating propeller, and with the suggestion of his friend, he met with Prof. Satish Dhawan for help. Prof. Dhawan told him to attend his class on Saturday from 2 pm - 3 pm for six weeks. Prof. Satish Dhawan prepared a schedule and gave him some reference material to prepare before the discussion on Saturday, Prof. (Dr) Dhawan used to ask the critical question to assess Prof. Abdul Kalam's depth. Prof. Abdul Kalam realized that a good teacher prepares himself with meticulous planning to teach and prepares the student to acquire knowledge. Prof. Abdul kalam got the capacity to design the contra-rotating propeller for hovercraft configuration. In the critical phases of testing, Prof. Dhawan witnessed the test. He congratulated Prof. Abdul Kalam for his success. According to Prof. Abdul Kalam, Prof. Dhawan was a visionary teacher who could link the student's dreams to manifestation.

6. To Develop Harmony in Society

"The teacher should not spread the poison of social inequality and communal intolerance in the minds of innocent children" (Kalam & Tiwari, 1999, p. 9). So teachers must be free irrespective of class, creed, gender, religion, etc., especially to encourage women's education for gender equality. So Prof. Abdul Kalam said that teachers should have just one vision to give the students the all-around capability, be creative and observant, acquire knowledge continuously, and be excellent performers with sterling character. The quality of a teacher is the passion for teaching, allowing thinking, and putting students' ahead, creating pressure to explore and free from communal mentality. Teachers must lead a life as noble people.

Message to the Teachers

i. Teachers must celebrate the success of students.
ii. Teachers must inspire children and guide them towards the mission of life.
iii. Teachers must provide them with value-based education
iv. The teacher must spread nobility in thinking and action among students,
v. Teachers must lead a noble lifestyle to transform lives.
vi. Teachers must treat all students equally and not discriminate based on sex, caste, religion or language.
vii. Teachers must be dedicated to their profession
viii. Teachers must maintain cordial inter-personal or intra-personal relationships with parents and the community.
ix. The teacher must have the vision to elevate average students.
x. Teachers must be autonomous learners and groom their students to become autonomous.
xi. Teachers must treat their students like their sons, daughters, grandsons or granddaughters.
xii. Teachers should identify the weak students in the class and be attentive to them.
xiii. Teachers should encourage all students to dream and transform dreams into thoughts and thoughts into action.

8

Teaching-Learning Methods

Prof. Abdul Kalam was in favour of inductive teaching methods such as discussion, the project method, excursions, and experimental teaching methods. he believed in nurturing children's capabilities and enabling them to solve problems with logical solutions satisfying their curiosity and answering their questions. To achieve this, both children and teachers need freedom in the teaching-learning process.

According to Prof. Abdul Kalam, one of the best learning methods is to follow up on behavioural patterns. Teachers' and parents' behaviour enlightens children to modify their behaviour. Learning by doing, i.e. the experimental method, should be followed in schools and colleges. Education must nurture the child's curiosity and integrate the thinking process, the skill of hands, mind and body. The problem-solving method should be given more emphasis. Self-observation outside the classroom is also important in the teaching-learning process. Prof. Abdul Kalam focused on the following areas in education.

i) Research and Enquiry,
ii) Creativity and Innovation,
iii) Capacity to use High-End Technology,
iv) Entrepreneurship and Moral leadership.

According to Prof. Abdul Kalam, question-answer, debating, discussion, lecture, demonstration, and experiment methods are to be used in teaching and learning.

Technology-Based Education: Prof. Abdul Kalam emphasised on tele-education, e-education for rural areas and the self-learning process. Prof. Abdul Kalam believed in technology-based teaching methods in education. Computers, laptops, mobile phones, tabs, and projectors are effective mediums of teaching-learning tools of education. Students can independently use the many where – in the classroom, hostel, at home or on the way. They can store different files and exchange and share opinions through email, chatting, messaging and WhatsApp. It gives them access to more knowledge and better communication with the universe. It is a self-learning process; through this e-learning method, students can complete assignments and submit them. Students learn individually through software. This method of teaching reduces time and distance. With this system, we can share all information on the hard disk. There is a need for a digital library system to access the required knowledge. Technology-enhancing learning is an attempt to develop knowledge through information and communication technology rapidly. It is most useful for distance mode of education and economically viable. Tele-education and virtual classrooms can enhance both the quality and quantity of education. Students must be encouraged to use the latest technology in education. Web-based e-learning programmes must be facilitated through internet service both for urban and rural areas. The Government of India; Ministry of Human Resource development has launched a programme called "Sakshat" for the same.

The nation must not deprive anyone of education regarding societal and economic discrimination. Prof. Abdul Kalam said, "A nation where the rural and urban divide has reduced to a thin line. A nation must provide equitable distribution and adequate access to energy and quality water, and the government must be responsive, transparent and corruption free. (Education should not be a business product, p. 2). Prof. Abdul Kalam suggested using the mobile laboratory to develop students of rural areas, particularly on holidays, to develop creativity and experiment-based learning. He also suggested developing a 'home library' system.

Concept of Students

Students are the centre point of Prof. Abdul Kalam's educational philosophy. He believed that "Students should never be made to wait" and did not want to be late to meet children and said to the students with a smile, 'Funny guys! Are you doing well?" Even at the final lecture in Shillong, on 27th July 2015, he said it for the last time. These were his last words before a long pause. He felt unwell and passed away forever.

According to Prof. A. P. J. Abdul Kalam-

1. The student should be an autonomous learner.
2. The student must be an active participant in awareness rallies, exhibitions, and activities for social development.
3. The student must be able to use modern technologies like computers and the internet.
4. Self-discipline, i.e., natural obedience, must be maintained by the students towards their elders.
5. The student must have the vision to build their future life (Kalam, 2003, Teachers should be role models).
6. Students must have entrepreneurial leadership to be employed independently and to fulfill the dream of a developed India by 2020.
7. Students should be careful about elderly family members, ailing and differently challenged people.
8. Students should share knowledge and skills with lacking students.
9. Students must be nature lovers and plant at least five plants in school or house to develop the environment.

Teacher-Student Relationship

Prof. Abdul Kalam's concept of teacher-student relationships can be understood using conceptual content analysis and the Exploratory Philosophical method. Prof. Abdul Kalam states, "Education and the teacher-student relationship have to be seen not in business terms but with the nation's growth in mind. A proper education would help nurture a sense of dignity and self-respect among our youth." (Kalam, 2002, p. 23) Prof. Abdul Kalam defined that education cannot be a business product. Education has to be delivered in an integrated way by great teachers through a good syllabus and with the affinity between parents, students and teachers (Education should not be a business product: p. 2). Prof. Abdul Kalam himself pointed out the teacher-student relationship from his practical life and said that "While working together on RATO motors and the Missile Panel, Narayanan and I played the roles of student and teacher interchangeably wherever required." (Kalam & Tiwari, 1999, p. 5) He said that his teacher Narayanan and Prof. Abdul Kalam in the project RATO motors and on the Missile panel worked interchangeably on the teacher-student relationship. So, the teacher-student relationship is a mutual understanding. Prof. Abdul Kalam believed in healthy and facilitated teacher-student relationships with the freedom of the child to explore themselves with the full faith of the teacher in his children with dignity and self-respect on either end. A teacher must patiently answer children's questions to satisfy their curiosity.

Concept of Parents

It is better to analyse Prof. Abdul Kalam's speeches to understand his views regarding the concept of parents in education through Conceptual content analysis and Thought experiment philosophical method. Prof. Abdul Kalam's father, Jainulabdeen, inspired him by saying, "This Island may be housing your body but not your soul. Your soul dwells in the house of tomorrow, which none of us at Rameswaram can visit, not even in our dreams. May God bless you, my child!" (Kalam & Tiwari, 1999, p. 11). According to Prof. Abdul Kalam, parents have an important role in making the child a good human being, hard-working, and enlightened citizen. They must keep close vigilance about their children's interests and abilities and let them access education and set an example of their good behaviour and conduct before the child so that the child can develop love and respect for them and follow them as their role models. They must create an atmosphere for the child to ask questions and communicate with them freely. In the adolescent period, the child demands freedom, forms peer groups, and tries to satisfy curiosity. Parents must pour their parental love and keep a close eye on them to discover any behavioural changes in their son/daughter and help them overcome the situation with their love and affection. They must have a keen interest in the health of their child as well as games and sports, fine arts, music, dance etc. Parents have to be careful of their children's attendance in school. So, the parents have the duty to transform their children into responsible citizens, allowing them to see dreams. So, parents must lead their children in education and guide them to become good human beings."Your children are not your children. They are the sons and daughters of Life's longing for itself. They come through you but not from you. You may give them your love but not your thoughts. For they have their own thoughts." (Kalam & Tiwari, 1999, p. 10). According to Prof. Abdul Kalam, children are the greatest wealth of the nation. They are like blossoms, happy and fresh. He appealed to their parents not to burden them with their frustrations and hopelessness and not pollute their pure minds. Prof. Abdul Kalam said, "It is very important for every parent to be willing to make an effort to guide children to be good human beings – enlightened and hard-working." (Kalam, 2002, p. 23). According to Prof. Abdul Kalam, India would get a new life if parents and teachers showed dedication to shaping their children's lives.

Concept of Educational Institution

The concept of the educational institution of Prof. Abdul Kalam is analysed through Concept analysis and Exploratory Philosophical methods. According to Prof. Abdul Kalam, a student completes up to 10+2 and spends 25,000 hours in school. To become a full-fledged responsible citizen and to be able to realize their dreams, students should be physically fit academically sound with capacities for research and inquiry, innovation in thought and work. A student should be able to use high-end technology and possess entrepreneurship and moral leadership qualities. Students should be emotionally mature and spiritually awakened. Education requires basic amenities like good buildings with proper lighting and ventilation, spacious and airy classrooms, a library, laboratories, availability of technology in education, safe drinking water, clean toilets, and a playground. Resource mobilization for the unprivileged section of society is needed for widespread education, particularly in rural and urban poor areas.

According to Prof. Abdul Kalam, the education system has to develop the five minds:

i. *The Disciplinary Mind:* to be a master of mind in different schools of thought like Science, Mathematics, and History and proficiency in at least one professional craft.
ii. *The Synthesising Mind:* to develop the ability to integrate different disciplines or spheres into a coherent form.
iii. *The Creative Mind:* to develop the capacity to uncover and clarify new problems, questions and phenomena.
iv. *The Respectful Mind:* to develop tolerance and appreciation for differences of opinion.
v. *The Ethical Mind:* to develop responsibility as a citizen.

Role of Educational Institutions in Education

- An educational institution (school/college/university) has to provide not only a degree but also make students experts in using technology to integrate education with occupation.
- An educational institution has to create an atmosphere where children can ask questions and get answers freely. Prof. Abdul Kalam recognised that his teacher Shri Subramania Iyer used to teach theoretical knowledge with practical examples. Once, he took all the students to the seashore of Rameswaram to explain birds flying. He showed how sea birds were flying with a marvelous formation of body position, flapping their wings with different positions of tail, body and head. All the students found that birds can fly as they desire and are powered by their own life and the motivation they want. At that very moment, Prof. Abdul Kalam finalised his future course of study as flight science. Prof. Abdul Kalam asked his teacher to tell him about the progress of further study in flight science. His teacher asked him to complete the school exam and go to college to study flight sciences. In 1954, Dr Abdul Kalam was admitted to MIT for aeronautical engineering and became a flight engineer in 1957. So the institution must ensure an atmosphere of asking questions to teachers and receiving answers.
- Educational institutions should develop creativity and constructiveness among students for global human development.
- Educational institutions must focus on igniting the minds of students. The educational centre should become a knowledge and skill centre.
- Heads of all academic institutions must be responsible for inspiring youth to study subjects of their interest.

- Prof. A. P. J. Abdul Kalam emphasised basic amenities like a Pucca school building with ventilated, lighted, airy and spacious classrooms, safe drinking water, clean toilets, and playgrounds in educational institutions. To assure this, all sponsoring authorities have to be justify that schools maintain some basic norms for their affiliation.
- Education institutions have to maintain content generalization and cost-effectiveness.
- Technological connectivity among universities and institutions has to be pursued for a global outlook. University education shall be made for the nation's sustainable development and to develop a "research spirit".
- The key points to enhance educational competencies are the home library concept and creative classrooms. Home libraries should be introduced for educational development on a personal level, even if it can be started with a few books. Using technology (ICT) and the active participation of students and teachers can transform a classroom into a creative classroom.
- Religious institutions- Prof. Abdul Kalam believed that each religion is similar regarding universal truth, i.e., the inner core concept (the basic spiritual unity) of all religions. It is the 'unity of minds' –in the diversity of rites, rituals, ideas and beliefs in men. Prof. Abdul Kalam suggested that religious, educational institutions should open enrolment to children from other religions to develop tolerance and spread the understanding of the unity of religions. Value-based educational material should be served. So, it will spread among the people that multiple religions are working together for the same goal, and it will reduce religious conflicts.

Educational institutions have to prepare enlightened citizens of the future with the ability to serve the nation. Science, technology and Government policy must be interrelated for the mutual benefit of human development. The institution has to maintain cost-effectiveness and content generation through virtual classrooms. Technological connectivity among universities and institutions has to be pursued for a global outlook. Dynamic institutions for quality teaching will be equipped with a library, internet, e-learning and modern laboratories to develop the sense of 'I can do it', 'We can do it' and "India can do it." Teachers of an educational institution must be role models in students' eyes and lead a noble life that will set a noble example before the students.

9
Women and Youth Education

Women Education

The concept of women's education by Prof. Abdul Kalam is analysed from the speeches and writings of Prof. Abdul Kalam through concept analysis and the Exegetical, Philosophical method. Prof. Abdul Kalam encouraged women's education for gender equality in society and the equal role of women in the transformation of the nation. According to Prof. Abdul Kalam, every organization has to be made aware that there is no difference between men and women. Women are equal partners in national development. He said if a mother is happy, the entire family is happy. If all the families are happy, the society will be healthy. If the society is healthy, the country will be strong and vibrant. The peace and prosperity of the nation depend on not only men but also women. According to Prof. Abdul Kalam, women's education must be prioritized. There is a need to ensure women's education in secondary and higher education. Distance education packages can be significant for women in remote areas. After completing primary general education, a girl can opt for a vocational training programme to enable her self-employment or employment in establishments. Emphasis should be given to making every woman educated and economically self-dependent. Prof. Abdul Kalam wanted a nation where crime against women and children is absent, and none in society feels alienated.

Youth Education

Relational content analysis, exploratory and critical philosophical analysis are used to analyse different speeches of Prof. Abdul Kalam to understand his view on youth education. Prof. Abdul Kalam said that the young mind sees their dream in sleep but does not let them sleep until they fulfill it. Prof. Abdul Kalam believed that India could transform itself into a developed nation and that the people of India could achieve the best in the world. They have a fantastic mix of belief and knowledge that sets them apart from other nations. He said, "Given the freedom to achieve and guided properly, I am convinced the young of India can accomplish far more." (Kalam 2002, Prelude p. x) According to Prof. Abdul Kalam, children and youth are the nation's powers. He always preferred to meet and motivate them. He asserted, "What they dream of can become possible, that they can have anything that comprises a good life: health, education, the freedom to pursue their goals, and above all, peace." (Kalam 2002, Prelude p. xi) He suggested for the youth by saying, "Thinking is the capital, Enterprise is the way, Hard work is the solution." (Kalam 2002, Prelude p. xii) Prof. Abdul Kalam's teacher Iyadurai Solomon taught him, "To succeed in life and achieve results, you must understand and master three mighty forces — desire, belief and expectation." His speech for the youth said that children and youth should see the dream and fulfill it into reality. Youth needed freedom "Given the freedom to achieve and guided properly, I am convinced the young of India can accomplish far more." (Kalam 2002, Prelude p. x)

"Dream, Dream, Dream
Dreams transform into thoughts
And thoughts result in action." (Kalam, 2002, p. 25)

It is pertinent to point out, "What they dream of can become possible, that they can have anything that comprises a good life: health, education, the freedom to pursue their goals, and above all, peace." (Kalam, 2002, Prelude. xi). According to Prof. Abdul Kalam, youth must commit to fulfilling their dream "I believe I can, then I acquire the ability to do" (Kalam, 2002, p. 19). He said, "Friends, if there are no dreams, there are no revolutionary thoughts; if there are no thoughts, no actions will emanate. Hence, parents and teachers should allow their children to dream." (Kalam, 2002, p. 25). He suggested, "Thinking is the capital, Enterprise is the way, Hard Work is the solution." (Kalam, 2002, Prelude. xii). So, children and youth should see the dream and fulfill it into reality.

According to Prof. Abdul Kalam, youth must commit to fulfilling dreams, "I do know is that there is no greater power in heaven or on earth than the commitment to dream. Dreams hold something of." (Kalam, 2002, p. 17). He recalls, "Whatever you can do or dream, you can begin it. Boldness has genius, power and magic in it. Begin it now. — Goethe" (Kalam, 2002, p. 36). He suggested with faith; you can change your destiny. "We need a spirit of victory, a spirit that will carry us to our rightful place under the sun, a spirit which can recognize that we, as inheritors of a proud civilization, are entitled to our rightful place on this planet." (Kalam, 2002, p. 44). Prof. Abdul Kalam pointed out that the motto of youth education is:

Awakening the feeling of honour, clarity of vision, the concept of freedom, guidance and self-respect among youngsters is the motto of education. Prof. Abdul Kalam believed that dreams transform into thoughts, thoughts move to action and thus ignited minds manifested by the full utilisation of human and material resources. It is also true that the great dream of a dreamer is always transcended.

Education turns youth towards industry and business with proper training and competences. India is the second largest country in the world with 65% (below 35 years) vibrant youth and 74.04% literary (census 2010-2011). According to Prof.

Abdul Kalam, education must be connected with productivity, i.e., to develop the ability to earn and nation development.

Prof. Abdul Kalam believes that only the teaching profession in the world is more important to society than any other profession. In 2001, Prof. Abdul Kalam took the mission of interacting with 40000 young students to share his experiences with them, helping them to ignite their imagination and preparing them to work for a developed India. Prof. Abdul Kalam met with students to share his experiences and motivate them to do something for the nation. Breathe passed away on 27th July 2015 among youths in Shillong, Manipur.

As a great teacher Prof. Abdul Kalam inspired the youth of the nation to contribute to nation-building and was in favour of democratic policies to address national problems. Prof. Abdul Kalam said, "My message, especially to the young people, is to have the courage to think differently, invent, travel the unexplored path, discover the impossible, conquer the problems, and succeed. These are great qualities that they must work towards. This is my message to the young people." (Rupainwar, appendix. Ph.D. Thesis, p. 225). He advised the young generation to convert negative energy and thoughts into positive energy.

Prof. Abdul Kalam stated that his senior colleagues discouraged him from dreaming big. He felt sad by the comments of his senior colleagues – "Many even called us a group of eccentric inventors in pursuit of an impossible dream. I, being the leader of the "navvies", was a particularly inviting target. I was regarded as another country bumpkin who believed riding the air was his domain. The weight of opinion against us buttressed my ever-optimistic mind" (Kalam & Tiwari, 1999, p. 28). Prof. Abdul Kalam said, "I told my colleagues, "Here is a flying machine, not constructed by a bunch of cranks but by engineers of ability. Don't look at it —it is not made to look at, but to fly with." (Kalam & Tiwari, 1999, p. 29). From his first year of study at MIT, Prof. Abdul Kalam used to see a rejected hovercraft standing idle on the college campus, and last of all, Prof. Abdul Kalam, with some of his friends, made it fly and overcame all sorts of criticism of his classmates. So, converting negative energy and thoughts into positive energy is the best policy.

Reading books fulfils the acquisition of knowledge and satisfies the curiosities of the young generation. The four books that inspired Prof. Abdul Kalam are (Kalam, 2002, p. 31):

i) 'Man the Unknown' by Nobel laureate Dr Alex Carrel helped Prof. Abdul Kalam to know how the mind and body are integrated;
ii) 'Thirukkural' by Tiruvalluvar helped him to know an excellent code of life.
iii) The book 'Light from Many Lamps' by Lillian Eicher Western taught him how to live.
iv) Finally the 'Holy Quran' shaped his life and vision.

10

Moral Value and Spiritual Education

Value Education

The concept of moral values education of Prof. Abdul Kalam is derived from his speeches and writings through conceptual analysis and the exegetical, philosophical method. According to Prof. Abdul Kalam, in his childhood, he had learned a great lesson from his father, Janab Avul Pakir Jainulabdeen. The lesson was that in his childhood, his father was elected as a Panchayat Board member as well as president of the Panchayat Board. One day the schoolboy Kalam was reading his lessons loudly in kerosene lamps, and his parents went to attend evening namaz. At that moment, someone came to their door and asked about his father and said he had brought something for him. In the absence of his parents, the child Kalam replied to leave the item on a cot. When his father came and saw a tambalun kept in the cot, a costly dhoti, angavastram, some fruits, some sweets and in a slip the name of the person who left all these. His father asked Kalam about the tambalun, and the child Kalam replied someone came and has kept it for you. His father got upset about such gifts, and though Kalam was the youngest and most loving child of his father, the child Kalam was thoroughly beaten up. After that, his father, Janab Avul Pakir Jainulabdeen, touched his shoulder with love and affection and advised him with an Islamic Hadith "When the Almighty appoints a person to a position, he takes care of his provision.

If a person takes anything beyond that, it is illegal again." A gift is always accompanied by some purpose and is like touching a snake and getting the position in turn. According to Manu Smriti, by accepting gifts divinity, that person gets extinguished and makes the person do something not according to law but in favour of that person who had served the gift. His father advised Prof. Abdul Kalam that he would be happy if he practiced it sincerely. This incident taught Prof. Abdul Kalam a moral lesson for a lifetime.

Prof. Abdul Kalam said, "I wish to live the rest of my life at peace with myself and others. I have no wish to engage in quarrels with others." (Kalam 2002, p. 85) He asserted that from the beginning, right from birth, people should be taught values; only then people will become virtuous. Prof. Abdul Kalam suggested, "We need people who live by the laws of the scriptures and bear faith in God." (Kalam 2002, p. 67) So, for the up gradation of society, education must provide moral values. In order to produce an enlightened citizen, a child must be nurtured with love and affection and must be provided with value-based education in school and family. A child born in a family — the unit of society, and moral values must be provided for the welfare of the family, society and nation to become an enlightened citizen. School education must have the priority to make them corruption free. Parents and teachers have a great impact on children. A child inherits the principles of values from parents and teachers and builds character within the family and school. So the motto of every parent is "I will make my home a righteous home." Moral education should be imparted in schools and colleges by the lecture of a great teacher once a week as a class of moral science to elevate our heritage, make up young minds to love the country, and love other human beings. It is said that if the child misses the value of education in school, the nation will lose an enlightened citizen.

Spiritualism Education

Relational content analysis and critical philosophical analysis are used to understand Prof. Abdul Kalam's concept of spiritualism. According to Prof. Abdul Kalam, "Each individual creature on this beautiful planet is created by God to fulfill a particular role. Whatever I have achieved in life is through His help and an expression of His will. He showered His grace on me through some outstanding teachers and colleagues, and when I pay my tributes to these fine persons, I am merely praising His glory. All these rockets and missiles are His work through a small person called Dr Abdul Kalam." (Kalam & Tiwari, 1999, p. xv). According to him, we are all born with a divine fire. Our efforts are to give wings to this fire and fill the world with the glow of goodness. In this context, Prof. Abdul Kalam's view is important. "I have endeavored to understand the fundamental truths revealed to me by my father and feel convinced that there exists a divine power that can lift one from confusion, misery, melancholy and failure and guide one to one's true place. And once an individual severs his emotional and physical bondage, he is on the road to freedom, happiness and peace of mind." (Kalam & Tiwari, 1999, p. 5) Dr Abdul Kalam was enlightened with the great epic the Ramayana and the prophet. He said, "Events from the Ramayana and the life of the Prophet were the bedtime stories; my mother and grandmother would tell the children in our family." (Kalam & Tiwari, 1999, p. 9) Prof. Abdul Kalam mentioned that there was a very old mosque in the locality where his father would take him for evening prayers. He had not the faintest idea of the meaning of the Arabic prayers chanted, but he was convinced that the prayer reached God. His father told him there was nothing mysterious about prayer; rather, prayer made them able to possibly commune with the spirit between people. He said when we pray, we transcend our body and become a part of the cosmos, which knows no division of wealth, age, caste, or creed. (Kalam & Tiwari, 1999,

p. 4) Prof. Abdul Kalam recalls his childhood and said, in his childhood, they circled around the Rameshwaram temple like other pilgrims and felt a flow of energy passing through them. "Circling around the temple with the same reverence as any pilgrim from a distant part of the country, we felt a flow of energy pass through us." (Kalam & Tiwari, 1999, p. 6) He was too liberal towards other religions and said, "I never doubted that the prayers in the temple reached the same destination as the ones offered in our mosque." (Kalam & Tiwari, 1999, p. 6)

Spirituality ignites our dormant inner energy and guides our lives. The radiance of such a mindset brings peace, prosperity and bliss to the nation. Prof. Kalam said, "I have always been religious in the sense that I maintain a working partnership with God. I was aware that the best work required more ability than I possessed, and therefore, I needed help that only God could give me" (Kalam & Tiwari, 1999, p. 49). Prof. Abdul Kalam also said that fulfilling a youth's dream requires an innate connection with spirituality and self-realisation, discovering the power within us. So, spirituality is the self-realisation or discovery of the power within.

Science and Spirituality

According to Prof. Abdul Kalam, scientists should become "civic scientists" and ensure that scientific results will enrich the common person. How man uses science to make it a blessing or a curse? For example, nuclear energy can be used to generate electricity and make bombs. Fertilisers can be used in agriculture to improve yield, while the same chemicals can also be used in chemical weapons. So it is one's choice. In this regard, he said, "As I look at it, the path of science can always wind through the heart. For me, science has always been the path to spiritual enrichment and self-realisation." (Kalam & Tiwari, 1999, p. 15) He explained that scientific temper must emerge from the heart and be connected with spirituality and self-realisation.

11
Karmayoga

Introduction

The term 'work' is synonymous with 'Karma'. Karma is derived from the Sanskrit word 'kri', and 'kri' means action, to do, a conscious voluntary activity. 'Yoga' means root/mode of action. So, karma-yoga refers to a path, work technique or law of action. According to karmayoga, where there is a cause, there is an effect. Karma is a purposeful activity.

Philosophy of Work

Prof. Abdul Kalam's philosophy of work is based on five principles of performance degraders, performance dimensions, communication, commitment and flow.

1. *Performance Degraders:* Performance degraders mean some persons do not work hard and take any responsibility rather than prevent others from doing any work. It is not desirable for that person and the country; it is inertia of negativity.
2. *Performance Dimension:* "Performance dimensions are factors that lead to creation. They go beyond competencies such as the skills and knowledge of the individual." (Kalam & Tiwari, 1999, p. 81).
3. *Communication:* Communication is a 'Mantre' to emphasis each team member to realize the organisation's goals, the role to play each person, understand the problem, and collectivity

to solve the issues. So communication is the relationship between each team member from top to bottom.

4. *Commitment:* Commitment refers to involvement with the work in a positive sense to do it or to be able to do it in any situation. Prof. Abdul Kalam did not bother about committing to do something. Sometimes he and his team worked till late at night.

According to Prof. Abdul Kalam, "flow" is a sensation that comes from experience when we act with total involvement. He said one could attain this flow through continuously being involved in a task, which is increased by analyzing behavior on occasion. It is a moment of magic, making one feel relaxed, energetic and fresh. It is a feeling that someone is performing a task better today than yesterday. Prof. Abdul Kalam maintained the work environment lively and ensured a good blend of the experiences of the old scientists with younger colleagues.

Strategy of Work

Prof. Abdul Kalam had the strong faith in the principle of "*Kalkare so aajkar, Aajkare so ab* (What you will do tomorrow do today; what you will do today, do it now)." (Nair, 2011, p. 13). He believed that goal setting, positive thinking, visualizing and believing are the four basic factors of successful outcomes and involvement, participation, and commitment are the keywords of successful functioning. "...the four basic factors that I am convinced are involved in successful outcomes: goal-setting, positive thinking, visualising, and believing" (Kalam & Tiwari, 1999, p. 60). So, the work strategy depends on goal setting, positive thinking, visualizing and believing. He believed that one must be determined to be single-minded in one's vision and keep all problems outside for a better work strategy. He said, "I would enter the assembly shop leaving my other problems outside, just as my father used to enter the mosque for prayer, leaving his shoes outside" (Kalam & Tiwari, 1999, p. 28). Prof. Abdul Kalam learned decision-making skills, leadership qualities, and spiritual understanding from his close observation of his father, brother-in-law –Jallaludin, teacher Lyadurai Solomon, Dr Sarabhai, Dr Satish Dhawan, Dr Bramprakash and even from his colleagues and subordinates working with him.

Goal Setting

Prof. Abdul Kalam always preferred to work within a schedule - "I used to prepare a general schedule during my morning walk and emphasized two or three things I would definitely like to accomplish during the day including at least one thing that would help achieve long-term goals" (Kalam & Tiwari, 1999, p. 69). In his autobiography, he pointed out, "Within the next ten minutes, I would scan all the papers and quickly divide them into different categories: those that required immediate action, low priority ones, ones that could be kept pending, and reading material." (Kalam & Tiwari, 1999, p. 69). He always wanted to complete his work before the stipulated time with great courage, dedication and motivation to achieve the goal. He believed that human beings are the creation of God and that to do anything, dreaming is the first priority. He indeed wanted to become a pilot, and finally, he became a pilot of pilots, satellites, missiles, atomic power and of the nation of India. According to the pragmatic theory, there is no difference between belief and action. Strong belief refers to goal setting in mind and with a commitment to achieve the goal.

It is pertinent to point out that Prof. Abdul Kalam, from a young age, observed seagulls flying on the seashore, and it made him realize his goal to be an aeronautical engineer. Prof. Abdul Kalam (1999) said, "Simple, provincial boy though I was, I was convinced that one day I, too, would soar up into the skies; indeed, I was the first child from Rameshwaram to fly." (Kalam & Tiwari, 1999, p. 13). He was a visionary and planned for India Mission 2020 and set the goal to harness collective energy for a broader purpose and greater benefit.

Positive Thinking

Prof. Abdul Kalam's supervisor and guide at MIT, Professor Srinivasan, was disappointed with his performance a week ago. He said he would like to see the work assigned to Abdul Kalam by Monday, (the next three days) otherwise, he would stop the scholarship of Abdul Kalam. One day before the deadline, during a surprise visit, Professor Srinivasan found that Abdul Kalam had done a great job with day and night continuous effort without any rest and completed the task with dedication. Professor Srinivasan appreciated Abdul Kalam for his work. Abdul Kalam realized that anything is possible if one wants to do anything with dedication and rigorous effort.

Prof. Abdul Kalam had a positive attitude and self-reliance to realize his dreams. He was dedicated to working within a work schedule, organising, coordinating and supervising work. "I used communication to promote understanding and to come to an agreement with colleagues in defining the problems that existed and in identifying the action necessary to be taken to solve them. Effective communication was one of the tools skillfully used in managing the project" (Kalam & Tiwari, 1999, p. 76). In DRDL, he usually arranged guest lectures by experts from IIT, CSIR (Council of Scientific and Industrial of Research), and TIFR (Tata Institute of Fundamental Research) to discuss work progress and to build up positive attitudes among colleagues. He periodically met with all scientists, juniors and seniors, veterans and freshers to positively follow up the project activities. He utilised 12 academic institutions, 30 laboratories of DRDO, CSFR and ISRO and the involvement of 50 professors and 100 research scholars to solve missile-related problems. He was a good listener who had the power to appreciate collective wisdom for success. It is pertinent to say that in his first year of study at MIT, Dr Abdul Kalam used to see a rejected hovercraft standing idle on the college campus. Prof. Abdul Kalam, with some of his friends, made it to fly and overcome all sorts of criticism from his classmates. Senior colleagues of Dr Abdul Kalam criticized and discouraged him from dreaming so highly of the Ground Equipment Machine (GEM) Project. Dr Abdul Kalam stated – "Many even called us a group of eccentric inventors in pursuit of an impossible dream. I, being the leader of the "navvies", was a particularly easy target. I was regarded as another country bumpkin who believed flying was his domain. The weight of opinion against us buttressed my ever-optimistic mind." (Kalam & Tiwari, 1999, p. 28). Dr Abdul Kalam transformed all these negative comments to positive energy among his teammates. He said Indians are suffering from huge problems due to a lack of clarity of vision and direction, suffering with misery due to their ignorance to manage and select "the next best alternative." It is called 'Psychological inertia." With a positive vision, Dr Abdul Kalam replied, "I told my colleagues, "Here is a flying machine, not constructed by a bunch of cranks but by engineers of ability. Don't look at it — it is not made to look at, but to fly with." (Kalam & Tiwari, 1999, p. 29).

Visualising

Visualising a clear idea is essential to achieve a goal. A practical example of Prof. Abdul Kalam is given below.

SLV-III (dream project of Dr Abdul Kalam) launch was scheduled on 10th August 1979 at 7:58 A.M. from Sriharikota, but in the second stage, it turned out of control and in 317 seconds, it crashed in to the Bay of Bengal, 560 kms away from Sriharikota. Prof. Satish Dhawan took responsibility for the failure, but as the project director, this failure was the failure of Prof. Abdul Kalam. In this context, Dr Abdul Kalam said, "I lost my launch vehicle in the sea but recovered successfully. Your missile is in front of you. In fact, you have lost nothing but a few weeks of work." (Kalam & Tiwari 1999, p. 150). Despite the failure of SLV-III Prof. Abdul

Kalam said, "SLV-III is a genuine Indian design, and you may be having your own troubles. But you should always remember that we don't just build on success, we also build on failures." (Kalam & Tiwari, 1999, p. 88) This was the clear vision to achieve the goal as part of Karmayoga. In another incident, Prof. Abdul Kalam's dream project, the Agni missile launch, was scheduled for 20th April 1989. Still, at T-14 second computer signaled to hold on to the project, and consequently, the project was postponed for that day due to irreversible internal power consumption. The launch was rescheduled on 1st May 1989, but at T-10 seconds computer signaled to hold on. Because one of the control components S-I –TVC, was not working. After the failure of Agni, Prof. Abdul Kalam said, "I promise you, we will be back after successfully launching Agni before the end of this month." (Kalam & Tiwari, 1999, p. 151) But on 22nd May 1989 Agni Missile launch was successful. Dr Abdul Kalam said, "A major achievement in our continuing efforts to safeguard our independence and security by self-reliant means. The technology demonstration through Agni reflects our commitment to the indigenous development of advanced technologies for the nation's defence." (Kalam & Tiwari, 1999, p. 153) The success of Agni was the continuous effort of the genius engineers of India regarding the Nation's security and self-reliance and reflection of the technological advancement of the Nation. According to Prof. Abdul Kalam, "We have talked about the importance of having a dream and of commitment, of hard work and having the spiritual strength to persevere through difficulties and failures." (Kalam 2002, p. 89). Prof. Abdul Kalam properly knows the desired goal and has a clear vision to achieve it through commitment, hard work and perseverance.

Believing

Prof. Abdul Kalam was very proud of his Nation. He concentrated on the success of the SLV Project, despite the pain of the death of his father, mother and cousin. Prof. Abdul Kalam launched SLV-3 on 18th July 1980 from the SHAR Rocket launching station, and India was empowered as the fifth country for satellite launch compatibility. Prof. Abdul Kalam's experience from ISRO helped him utilize combined efforts in DRDL for the success of IGMDP. His dream project "Agni" missile was launched on 22nd May 1989. He said, "It is fire, in the heart of an Indian ... as it clings to the burning pride of this nation." (Kalam & Tiwari, 1999, p. 15). In this regard, former President R. Venkataraman said it was a tribute to the dedication, hard work and talent of Prof. Abdul Kalam. It has shown that Indians can develop using advanced technology to tackle real-life problems.

In the Bhagavad Gita, Chapter III, verse -700, Lord Shree Krishna told Arjuna that the ultimate goal of human life is liberation (moksha) from the bondage of birth and death attainment of bliss (Satchidananda), and the feeling of identity with *jiva* and Brahman. However, every action has its result, and one must accept it. Lord Krishna suggested that *Jivas* (human-being) should perform *karma* (duty) without attachment to there ward. Potentially all *jiva* is divine in nature, and we should perform our duty without being guided by the reward, as we have the right tokarma, not its result onlyfor selfless service. Therefore, surrender to completely to God, keep your trust in Him, and perform selfless activities.

According to *Bhagavad Gita*, Chapter III, Lord Shree Krishna pointed out - 'Karmanyevadhikaraste, ma phaleshu kadachana (you have the right to perform your duty but not to the fruits of action)'. So, karma-yoga is a mental discipline to serve duty as selfless service in the path of enlightenment.

According to Buddhism, Karma-yoga refers to practicing living on the eight-fold path – right speech, thought, perception etc. According to Buddhism, each and every action has a result. Karmais driven by *chetana* (intention) expressed through bodily karma, verbal karma, and mental karma. Practicing the eight-fold path can overcome the result of karma.

According to Swami Vivekananda, he works best who does not work for any motive, money, fame or anything else. Swami Vivekananda puts the example of karma-yoga based on practical Vedanta. Swami Vivekananda says, "To work, we have the right, but not to the fruits thereof. Don't think about the result if you want to do great work. Karmayoga is a selfless activity by the human being as it's divine nature.

Failures Management

It is said that one's caliber is tested not through his success but in failure management. According to Prof. Abdul Kalam, problems are part of life, and he has faced many problems.

Prof. Abdul Kalam said, "I was unaware of any other option for higher education. Nor did I have any information about career opportunities available to a student of science." (Kalam & Tiwari, 1999, p. 16) It means he had no idea of higher education and chose the subject of higher study for career opportunities. Prof. Abdul Kalam also said, "... but admission to this prestigious institution was an expensive affair around a thousand rupees was required, and my father could not spare that much money." (Kalam & Tiwari, 1999, p. 16) He had no financial capacity for admission to MIT, Madras. All these reflect his financial problems, but he managed the problem and reached his desired goal. In this situation, his sister Zohare financially helped him by mortgaging her gold ornaments, and Prof. Abdul Kalam was admitted to MIT, Madras.

Prof. Abdul Kalam was extremely disappointed to lose the opportunity to join the Indian Air Force (IAF), Dehradun, in his first interview for the job he liked to be a pilot. In this regard, Prof. Abdul Kalam said, "I could only finish ninth in the batch of 25 examined to select eight officers for commissioning in the Air Force. I was deeply disappointed" (Kalam & Tiwari, 1999,

p. 24). He was placed in the ninth position in the recruitment panel, from which the first eight candidates were selected to join the IAF.

Prof. Abdul Kalam was deeply saddened by the premature death of his dream project Nandi. He put his heart and soul into the Nandi project, but the government of India postponed the project. In this regard, he said, "It was a great shock, making me relive the earlier disappointments at Dehra Dun when I failed to get into the Air Force, and at Bangalore, when the Nandi project was aborted at ADE." (Kalam & Tiwari, 1999, p. 60)

Prof. Abdul Kalam said dedication to work, tolerance and taking responsibility, and utilization of team efforts and skills is the way to achieve the goal. Prof. Abdul Kalam said he worked with many people and organisations, and he had gladness to deal with these people. He said his colleagues were highly talented and rebellious, and they discussed different matters very enthusiastically, and the final decision was made. With Sarabhai's inspiration, Prof. Abdul Kalam searched for a way to build leaders who could elucidate the goals, their missions larger than their lives, and could then inspire their entire workforce (Kalam & Tiwari, 1999, p. 113). The goal was to harness the team's energy and visualize the goal through a collaborative strategy. (Rupainwar, 2016)

Summary

So, Prof. Abdul Kalam was a great leader, motivator, project director, engineer, scientist, poet, and ideal teacher with good art, literature and music knowledge. He was a nature lover, environmentalist and enjoyed classical music and used to play the vena. He respected all religions and recited the Holy Quran and the Bhagavad Gita daily. He enjoyed gardening, morning walks, yoga and prayers. He believed serving humanity was the way to lead a peaceful life. He inculcated the spirit of integrity, unity, teamwork, and honesty among young students to cherish their dreams. He said, "I have acquired nothing, built nothing, possess nothing, no family, sons and daughters" (Kalam & Tiwari, 1999, p. 177). He devoted his life to technological self-sufficiency. He was an obedient son, a good friend, a sincere student and a visionary teacher. (Rupainwar, 2016). He believed that a proper education system must have the vision to develop a sense of dignity, self-respect, quality citizen, and research mind for nation-building. He suggested, "Five important areas to transform India—education and healthcare, agriculture, information and communication, infrastructure and critical technology." (Kalam 2002, p. 67). Bama, a Tamil writer in her work "Karukku" (1992), illustrated how education can help one rise from a deep well, a metaphor for Prof. Abdul Kalam's journey from a poor village boy to becoming the 'Missile Man' (Rupainwar, 2016).

12

Abdul Kalam and Swami Vivekananda

A Comparative Study of Educational Philosophy

Introduction

The educational philosophies of Swami Vivekananda in the 19th century and Prof. Abdul Kalam in the 20th century as well as the 21st century, have a great impact on educational philosophy in the present context. Swami Vivekananda and Prof. Abdul Kalam have emphasized educational opportunities irrespective of class, creed, sex and economic status. They are true patriots, great teachers, and worldly accepted for their orthodox philosophy. Man is the centre point of their philosophy.

Similarities

Both Prof. Abdul Kalam and Swami Vivekananda believed that education manifests hidden power from within. According to Prof. Abdul Kalam education is "...one's communion with an eternal source of hidden knowledge within oneself — which each individual is bidden to seek and find for himself or herself" (Kalam & Tiwari, 1999, Prelude p. x). So, education is self-realisation. Similarly, Swami Vivekananda states, "Education is the manifestation of the perfection already in man" (Swami Vivekananda, 1972, Vol. 4, p. 358).

Prof. Abdul Kalam and Swami Vivekananda were supporters of nationalism. They were proud to be Indian and recognized the strength of India. They believed that the Indian people had immense capability to lead the world. Prof. Abdul Kalam said, "The nation is bigger than any individual" (Kalam 2002, p. 180) and concentrated on developing the competencies of our country. Prof. Abdul Kalam was delighted with the success of SLV-III (1980), the launching of the Agni missile in 1989 by DRDO the nuclear power test in 1998, and the development of the Kalam-Raju stent, Kalam-Raju tablet computer, and the formation of PURA. These are key points of his nationalistic attitude. Swami Vivekananda and Prof. Abdul Kalam are true patriots and nationalists. Similarly, according to Swami Vivekananda, Let New India arise in your place. Let her arise out of the peasant's cottage, grasping the plough, out of the huts of the fisherman, cobbler, and sweeper. Let her spring from the grocer's shop, from beside the oven of the fritter-seller. Let her emanate from the factory, from marts, and markets. Let her emerge from groves and forests, from hills and mountains. These common people have suffered oppression for thousands of years – suffered it without a murmur, and as a result have developed wonderful fortitude" (Swami Vivekananda, 2005, Vol. 7, p. 327).

The Philosophies of both Prof. Abdul Kalam and Swami Vivekananda are a coherent blend of Idealism, Realism, Naturalism, Humanism and Pragmatism

Idealism

Prof. Abdul Kalam said, "We are all born with a divine fire in us. Our efforts should be to give wings to this fire and fill the world with the glow of its goodness" (Kalam & Tiwari, 1999, Prelude p. xvi). He also mentioned, "I had been taught that true reality lay beyond the material world in the spiritual realm. And that knowledge could be obtained only through inner experience" (Kalam & Tiwari, 1999, Prelude p. 19). The terms 'divine fire in us', 'faith in God' 'reality lay beyond the material' and 'inner experience' refer to Prof. Abdul Kalam's Idealistic approach.

Swami Vivekananda defined education as "Education is the manifestation of the perfection already in man" (Swami Vivekananda, 1972, Vol. 4, p. 358) and "All knowledge and all powers are within. What we call power; secrets of nature and force are all within. All knowledge comes from the human soul. Man manifests knowledge, discovers it within himself, which is pre-existing through eternity" (Swami Vivekananda, 2018, Vol. 1, p. 422). "All knowledge, therefore, secular or spiritual, is in the human mind. In many cases, it is not discovered but remains covered, and when the covering is slowly removed, we say, "We are learning." (Swami Vivekananda, 2018, Vol. 1, p. 30). The terms 'already in man', 'all powers are within', 'knowledge comes from the human soul', 'within himself' and 'in the human mind' refer to the Idealistic approach of Swami Vivekananda.

Realism

Realism emphasizes useful and purposeful education for individual and social development using material resources to solve real-life problems. Prof. Abdul Kalam said, 'Educationists should build the capacities of the spirit of inquiry, creativity, entrepreneurial and moral leadership among students and become their role model." He also stated, "The entire education system is focused on five components: research and inquiry, creativity and innovation, capacity to use high-end technology, entrepreneurship and moral leadership." Therefore, education is to cope up with the practical problems of life. Both Swami Vivekananda and Prof. Abdul Kalam are realistic philosophers. According to Swami Vivekananda's speech "we want that education by which character is formed, the strength of mind is increased, the intellect is expanded, and by which one can stand on one's own feet". (Swami Vivekananda. 1989, Vol. 5. p. 342).

Naturalism

Prof. Abdul Kalam advocated for the full freedom of children in learning and development. He believed that the child is the centre point of education, emphasized the child's interests and tendencies, and stressed drawing out creative and innovative ideas. Swami Vivekananda stated, "You cannot teach a child anymore than you can grow a plant. All you can do is on the negative side, you can only help. It is a manifestation from within; it develops its own nature- you can only take away obstructions" (Swami Vivekananda. 1972, Vol. 4. p. 55). So, they are naturalists.

Humanism

Prof. Abdul Kalam's view is that "What they dream of can become possible, that they can have anything that comprises a good life: health, education, the freedom to pursue their goals, and above all, peace" (Kalam, 2002, Prelude. xi). Swami Vivekananda states, "The education which does not help the common mass of people to equip themselves for the struggle for life, which does not bring out the strength of character, a spirit of philanthropy, and the courage of a lion – is it worth the name? Real education enables one to stand on one's own legs" (Swami Vivekananda. 2005, Vol. 7, pp. 147-148). He also said, "If one religion is true, then all the others must be true." (Swami Vivekananda. 2018, Vol. 1. Prelude. xii) All these are signs of their humanistic approach.

Pragmatism

According to Prof. Abdul Kalam, "When troubles come, try to understand the relevance of your sufferings. Adversity always presents opportunities for introspection." (Kalam & Tiwari, 1999, p. 5). "I believe I can, then I acquire the ability to do" (Kalam, 2002, p. 19). These statements deny the difference between belief and action as well as support his pragmatic approach. Swami Vivekananda states, "Education is not the amount of information that is put into your brain and runs riot there, undigested, all your life. We must have life-building, man-making, and character-making assimilation of ideas. If you have assimilated five ideas and made them your life and character, you have more education than any man who has got by heart a whole library." (Swami Vivekananda, 1962, Vol. 3, p. 302). This reflects the pragmatic attitude of Swami Vivekananda and Prof. Abdul Kalam.

Relationship between Parents, Students and Teachers

Prof. Abdul Kalam and Swami Vivekananda have emphasized the importance of the relationship between parents, students and teachers in education.

Parents

According to Prof. Abdul Kalam, "Your children are not your children. They are the sons and daughters of Life's longing for itself. They come through you but not from you. You may give them your love but not your thoughts. They have their own thoughts" (Kalam & Tiwari, 1999, p. 10). "It is very important for every parent to be willing to make an effort to guide children to be good human beings – enlightened and hard-working" (Kalam, 2002, p. 23). So, it follows that parents must be positive and sincere in their child's education. According to Swami Vivekananda, "Negative thoughts weaken men. Do you not find that where parents are constantly taxing their sons to read and write, telling them they will never learn anything, and calling them fools and so forth, the latter does turn out to be so in many cases? If you speak kind words to boys and encourage them, they are bound to improve in time. What holds good for children also holds good for children in the region of higher thoughts. If you can give them positive ideas, people will grow up to be men and learn to stand on their own legs." (Swami Vivekananda, 2005, Vol. 7, p. 170).

Students

Prof. Abdul Kalam states, "The bond between the teacher and the taught ....is peculiar to India. The teacher is not a man, who comes just to teach me, and I pay him so much, and there it ends. In India, it is really like an adoption. The teacher is more than my father; I am his child, his son in every respect. I owe him obedience and reverence before my Father even; they say the Father gave me this body, but he showed me the way to salvation; he is greater than Father. And we carry this love, this respect for our teacher all our lives." (Swami Vivekananda, 2005, Vol. 8, p. 78). Prof. Abdul Kalam also said, "I said, 'When you are growing up, say till the age of fifteen, the best role model I can think of would be your father, your mother and your school teachers." (Kalam, 2002, p. 22). In this regard, it is pertinent to say, "While working together on RATO motors and the Missile Panel, Narayanan and I played the roles of student and teacher interchangeably wherever required" (Kalam & Tiwari, 1999, p. 5). So, the affinity of student, parents and teacher is needed in education. According to Swami Vivekananda, "My idea of education is Gurugriha-vasa. Without the personal contact of a teacher, there would be no education." (Swami Vivekananda, 2005, Vol. 5, p. 224). Because the core of teacher-student relations is maintained in this education system. According to Swami Vivekananda, the teacher must have no selfish desire for money or fame. "We should see that he does not teach with any ulterior motive, for name, or fame, or anything else, but simply for love, pure love for you. When spiritual forces are transmitted from the teacher to the taught, they can only be conveyed through the medium of love; there is no other medium that can convey them" (Swami Vivekananda, 2005, Vol. 4, p. 27)

Both of them inspired children and young.

Prof. Abdul Kalam inspired the young generation, saying, "Dream is not that which you see while sleeping; it is something that does not let you sleep." Similarly, Prof. Abdul Kalam inspired youth and children and said, Friends, if there are no dreams, there are no revolutionary thoughts; if there are no thoughts, no actions will emanate. Hence, parents and teachers should allow their children to dream." (Kalam 2002, p. 25). Youth must commit to fulfilling dreams - "I believe I can, then I acquire the ability to do" (Kalam, 2002, p. 19). He suggested for the youth, saying, "Thinking is the capital, Enterprise is the way, Hard Work is the solution." (Kalam 2002, Prelude. xii). Swami Vivekananda motivated youth by saying, arise, awake and stop not till the goal is reached. Swami Vivekananda states, "...stand up, be bold, be strong. Take the whole responsibility on your shoulders and know that you are the creator of your destiny" (Swami Vivekananda, 1972, Vol. 2, p. 225).

Both of them emphasized women's education. According to Prof. Abdul Kalam,"When the mother is educated, two families are educated. We want a nation where crimes against women and children are absent, and none in society feels alienated." According to Swami Vivekananda, "The mother is the one wing of a flying bird –the nation. There is no chance of the welfare of the world unless the condition of women is improved. It is not possible for a bird to fly on one wing" (Swami Vivekananda, 1993, rpt, 2008, p. 69).

Swami Vivekananda was a disciple of Sri Ramakrishna and was inspired by the religious guru. He served the world through Belur Math and Mission and led a monk's life. On the other hand Prof. Abdul Kalam was inspired by his parents, school teachers and college professors. He was also blessed by Swami Pramukh Maharaj of Swaminarayan Sanstha of Ahmedabad, Khwaja Moinuddin Chishti of Ajmer and Sankaracharya of Kanchi. He served the nation through DRDO, NASA, nuclear power development and as the President of India. Dr Abdul Kalam led a family life without a wife, son or daughter.

Both believed in sharing Western science to develop science education in India. Prof. Abdul Kalam visited the NASA Langley Research Centre (LRC) in Pognoson, Virginia,

Goddard Space Flight Center (GSFC) and Sounding Rocket Launching Station in 1963-64 for the experience of science and technology.

Swami Vivekananda wanted to send some young graduates to Japan to learn to use technology and to apply the same in India for the development of domestic production and self-employment.

Prof. Abdul Kalam advised us to move to rural areas with a mobile laboratory to provide rural students with practical knowledge. Swami Vivekananda wanted to spread science education in rural areas and suggested to move for rural areas with a globe and lantern to teach them science almost after a hundred years.

Prof. Abdul Kalam also wanted to deliver science education in the mother tongue at least up to the tenth class. Swami Vivekananda wanted to deliver science education in the mother tongue so that one can understand it easily.

Both believed that science and spirituality are correlated or complementary. Science and spirituality are complementary - both correlate science and spirituality.

According to Prof. Abdul Kalam, science and religion take us toward the truth and reality of life. God is important for spirituality, and science is important for material progress. Both are important in life. In this regard, the researcher pointed out, "As I look at it, the path of science can always wind through the heart. For me, science has always been the path to spiritual enrichment and self-realisation." (Kalam & Tiwari, 1999, p. 15). According to Abdul Kalam, scientific temper must emerge from the heart and be connected with spirituality and self-realisation. Swami Vivekananda realized that science does not contradict the eternal spiritual principle, but science and religion are concerned with truth. Science is involved in discovering the truth of the physical world, and religion tries to find the truth in the spiritual realm. So religion and science are complementary.

(Gupta, 2017, Comparative view of Education: On the light of Swami Vivekananda and Rishi Aravinda, Vol: 3, Issue-6, pp. 1-15) The researcher pointed out that according to Swami Vivekananda, spirituality is not just ritual; spirituality is life. According to Swami Vivekananda, spirituality is the science of the soul. (Swami Vivekananda, 2005, Vol 3, p. 160.) The ultimate aim of education is to transform a person into a spiritual one.

Both believed that teaching is selfless activity.

Similarly, according to Prof. Abdul Kalam, education is not a business product. The researcher pointed out, "Education and the teacher-student relationship must be seen not in business terms but with the nation's growth in mind. A proper education would help nurture a sense of dignity and self-respect among our youth." (Kalam, 2002, p. 23). According to Swami Vivekananda, teachers must have no selfish motive for money or fame. "We should see that he does not teach with any ulterior motive, for name, or fame, or anything else, but simply for love, pure love for you. When spiritual forces are transmitted from the teacher to the taught, they can only be conveyed through the medium of love; no other medium can convey them" (Swami Vivekananda, 2005, Vol. 4, p. 27).

Both Prof. Abdul Kalam and Swami Vivekananda believed that learning comes through mistakes or failure. At MIT, Dr Abdul Kalam was assigned by Dr Srinivasan, the director of MIT, to complete a drawing for the aerodynamics of a low-level attack aircraft. One day (Friday), Prof. Srinivasan examinedthe design and was disappointed with his performance. This incident made Prof. Abdul Kalam determined to prove himself. The day after, Prof. Srinivasan hugged him affectionately for his performance. In 1979, the SLV-III project was dropped in the Bay of Bengal, but in July 1980, SLV-III succeeded. So, in a realistic approach, education is a process to overcome failure. He defined F. A. I. L. as the First Attempt in Learning.

Similarly, "In language and literature, in poetry and the arts, in everything, we must point out not the mistakes that people are making in their thoughts and actions, but how they gradually are able to do these things better" Swami Vivekananda, (2005), Vol. 7, p. 170). The child should be allowed to make mistakes in the teaching-learning process to learn from them.

Dissimilarities

1. Prof. Abdul Kalam worked for material growth, and Swami Vivekananda worked for spiritual growth.
2. Prof. Abdul Kalam created weapons of destruction and believed in Jagata Satya and the existence of God. Swami Vivekananda fought against the world's falsehood; he believed in Brahmn Satya Jagat Mithya.
3. Prof. Abdul Kalam believed in religion for unity in diversity, while Swami Vivekananda believed in religion for peace and brotherhood.
4. Prof. Abdul Kalam believed in individual differences in the material world. Swami Vivekananda denies the individual differences. Prof. Abdul Kalam believed in individual differences in the material world. According to Swami Vivekananda, all we are identical to one and only Brahman; one is real, and many are unreal.
5. Prof. Abdul Kalam leads people to a dignified life. Swami Vivekananda leads people to renunciation. According to Prof. Kalam, the goal of life from a materialistic view is to live a dignified life, but according to Swami Vivekananda, moksha (salvation) is the Sumumbonum of life—the attainment of oneness with Brahman
6. Prof. Abdul Kalam believes in questioning, discussion, project, and experiment-based learning methods. Swami Vivekananda believes that nothing can be taught; everyone learns from within. He also recommended Gurugriha-vas,

lecture method, question-answer method of teaching and practical skill-based training as a learning process.

7. According to Prof. Abdul Kalam, the curriculum of study includes mother tongue, academic subjects with training skills inentrepreneurship. At the end of education, students will be awarded an academic certificate with a certificate of entrepreneurship (Teachers should be role models –http://creative.snlekha.com). According to Swami Vivekananda Curriculum of study are—mother tongue, classical language, international language, mathematics, science, hygiene, history, geography, physical education, morals, theology, the preaching of saints, religious books, and training skills (Para vidya and Apara vidya).
8. On the other hand, Prof. Abdul Kalam's philosophy of education is reflected in Right to Education Act 2009. Swami Vivekananda's concept of education is reflected in Delors Commission Report - four pillars of education.
9. Other hand, Prof. Abdul Kalam advocated for science education and technology for a higher level of supremacy in the universe, employment in practical fields and training in schools and colleges. Swami Vivekananda advocated for vocational training for self-employment and the development of domestic products.
10. Prof. Abdul Kalam laid more emphasis on supremacy over the world through the development of science and technology. He said, "The new India will emerge out of the combination of biotechnology, biosciences, agriculture sciences and industrial development." (Kalam, 2002, p. 106). He emphasised—"Agriculture and food, Area of power, Electricity, Education and Healthcare, Information technology." (Kalam, 2002, p. 127). Prof. Abdul Kalam wanted to develop Space science (NASA), weapons for the military (DRDO) and Atomic energy (Nuclear power) along with biotechnology, bio-science, agricultural science,

electricity, health care and information technology for supremacy around the globe.

On the other hand, Swami Vivekananda has emphasized domestic production and employment generation more through the development of science and practical training based education.

11. Prof. Abdul Kalam has emphasized employment generation in training institutes, technical colleges and universities to develop skilled persons for massive employment in industries. Swami Vivekananda laid more emphasis on training the younger generation to contribute to domestic products.
12. Prof. Abdul Kalam laid emphasis on the digital classroom, virtual classroom, web-conferences, the use of the internet, well-equipped laboratories, libraries, and the use of CAL (Computer Assisted Learning) for science education. In the learning situation, Swami Vivekananda emphasized discipline, concentration of mind, knowledge of physics, astronomy, geography and training skills for science education.
13. Prof. Abdul Kalam wanted to develop science at a higher level with the advancement of technology for supremacy around the globe. On the other hand, Swami Vivekananda wanted to develop basic sciences among the youth of the nation for survival.
14. For Prof. Abdul Kalam, science education is for material prosperity and development of creativity. (https://www.quora.com/whatare the similarities between Dr Abdul Kalam and Swami Vivekananda?). For Swami Vivekananda, science for survival and spiritual development is a manifestation of hidden potentiality. He said that spirituality is the science of religion.

13

Abdul Kalam and Rabindranath Tagore

A Comparative Study of Educational Philosophy

Education is a fundamental process to change a man into a complete man through all-round development– physical, mental, social, emotional, moral, and spiritual as well as expected changes in behaviour and preparing one for the service of the nation.

Biswakabi, Kabiguru, Rabindranath Tagore, the first Nobel laureate in Asia (1913), was born on 7th May 1861 in an affluent family to father Maharshi Debendra-nath Tagore and Mother Sarala Debi, at Jorasako Thakurbari, Kolkata. He was influenced by his father and deeply ingrained in the Veda and Upanishads. Although he had not write any specific book on education, his educational thoughts were reflected in his writings, biographies, letters, novels, short stories, dramas etc. He is known as a Philosopher, Thinker, Educationist, Social activist, Visionary, Intellectual and a great Preacher of Indian culture and tradition in the 20th century. His educational philosophy is reflected in art, music, drama, literature, painting and the concept of social construction. He believed that education is the mental and physical training to manifest the innate capabilities of students. Shantiniketan (22nd December 1901) and Visva-Bharati (22nd September 1921) are two practical models of educational system of R. N. Tagore with equal importance on science and knowledge.

As a Vedantist, he believed in the concept of'I am Brahma'. Vedanta's core concept says, "Brahman Satya Jagat Mithya, Jiva

Brahmaiva Na Aparah." There is a spiritual bond between man and Brahman, and as the concept of 'Amritasya Putra,' there is a bond between man and man. It is pertinent to say, "Fortunately for me, I was brought up in a family where Literature, music and art had become instinctive. My brothers and cousins lived in the freedom of ideas, and most had natural artistic powers. Nourished in these surroundings, I began to think early and to dream and put my thoughts into expression. In religious and social ideas, our family was free from all conventions being ostracized by society owing to our secession from orthodox beliefs and customs. This made us fearless in our freedom of mind, and we tried experiments in all aspects of life" (Tagore, 1917, pp. 169-170)

1. Definition of Education

"The highest education is that which does not merely give us information but makes our life in harmony with all existence" said Rabindranath Tagore. R. N. Tagore believed that education is not acquiring some amount of information but making our life in harmony with all existence. It is the widest road to solve all our problems. At least the first twelve years child's mind must be educated with its natural tendencies and instincts. Only then will books be introduced. Naturalistic and aesthetic values mark Tagore's theory of education. Education leads one to culminate the realisation of the Universal man. Tagore laid emphasis on the intellectual, physical, social, moral, economic and spiritual aspects of human life by which a man can develop an integrated personality (https://www.academia.edu/4659110/Rabindranath_Tagore_on_Education). Tagore also believed that education must focus on economic upliftment, because economic life covers the whole width of the fundamental basis of society. He suggested educational institutions must have close associations with this economic life to obtain their fullness of truth. "Our university must not only instruct, but live; not only think, but produce" (https://archive.org/stream/-tagorehiseducati00jala/jala_djvu.txt).

As a humanist, he admitted on universal brotherhood and spiritual bondage of the universe, and the aim of education is to develop, i.e. physical, intellectual, and spiritual development of man. As an individualist, Tagore believed that every child has his/her inborn ability, which makes him/her unique qualities compared to others. He emphasized *tapasya* and *sadhana* as an ideals to shape their lives. As a naturalist, he laid emphasis on the utilization of the various elements in our environment so that one could be able to understand the subject in an effective manner. It is also true that education cannot flourish appropriately in a rigid classroom environment. It requires an open environment, just like the Gurukul system, where people learn through their own experiences from nature because God has created nature. If one is synchronised with nature, it means synchronised with God. Freedom is necessary for the all-round development of the learners.

2. Aims of Education

According to R.N. Tagore, education aims to develop spiritual qualities like discipline, tolerance, and courtesy and draw out the latent potentialities of children in a more lively and enjoyable manner. He has emphasised the development of literature, art and science as well as the development of villages and humankind to overcome animal nature and attain humanism. True education is the development of self-reliance, training young minds of men and women in freedom and strength, language and service.

Self-realisation: realization of one's own potential and full awareness of one's existence in relation to the experience of the outer world as well as the feeling of a core relationship with the universal spirit—God

Intellectual development: development of thoughts, imagination, creativity, curiosity and freedom.

Physical development: exercising through yoga, games and sports.

Humanity and universal brotherhood: international understanding around the Globe

Natural growth: growth in and with nature.

Freedom- freedom of head, heart-thought, will and expression.

Moral and Spiritual development: the value of appreciation, development of honesty, the mentality of sharing, caring and cooperation.

Social development: maintains the value the social relation and maintains the core relation service to man and service to God.

3. Curriculum

R. N. Tagore suggested that the curriculum include English, Bengali, Sanskrit, Arithmetic, History, Geography, and Science. The curriculum includes subjects such as mother tongue, other Indian languages and foreign languages, mathematics, natural sciences, health education, social sciences, agriculture, technical subjects, skill-oriented subjects, art, music, dance, philosophy, psychology, religion, excursions, and yoga. The mother tongue is the true vehicle of self-expression; people freely express their thoughts through mother tongues. So the medium of instruction should be the mother tongue. The pupils had to do all domestic work like housekeeping, gardening, and cooking. Life was simple, regular and austere and was inspired by the ideals of hospitality, self-help and respect for the elders. (https://archive.org/stream/tagore hiseducati00jala/tagorehiseducati00jala_djvu.txt).

4. Quality of a Teacher

R. N. Tagore believed that ideal education is possible only with ideal teachers. An ideal teacher must possess the following qualities:

i. Great love, affection and sympathy for the innocent child.

ii. Teachers should provide a conducive environment for children to perform constructive activities and learn through their own experiences.
iii. Teachers must involve students in constructive activities and inspire them to make a continuous effort.
iv. Teachers must have the capacity to enhance the abilities of learners and to realize their uniqueness.
v. The teacher must lead the child towards perfection and harmony.

5. Quality of Students

Rabindranath Tagore was aware of the qualities of the student as he said, "In our school, the boys rise very early in the morning before it is light. They attend to the drawing of water for their bath. They make up their beds. They do all those things that tend to cultivate the spirit of self-help" (Tagore, 1917, 176). Even he thought that there was a need for meditation in education. In this connection, he said, ". . . it is absolutely necessary for their mental health and development that they must not have more schools for their lesson, but a world whose guiding spirit is personal love" (Tagore, 1917, pp. 178-179) Rabindranath Tagore was opposed to the book-based education system.

In his story 'Tota Kahini' (Parrot Story), he argues against book-centric education because it leads students to intellectual death by swallowing dry knowledge like a bird in a cage (http://bn.m.wikipedia.org). On the other hand, his short story 'Chhuti'(Holiday) picturises the upbringing of a normal child in an urban chemical environment. The environment is far removed from nature leading the child not only to take a holiday from the urban mechanical world but also a permanent holiday from the world. According to Rabindranath Tagore "Education is learned only when it is imparted through the path of freedom" (https://archive.

org/stream/tagorehiseducati00jala/_djvu.txt). According to Rabindranath Tagore, "freedom is absolutely necessary for the intelligent growth of the mind as well as for the sweet nature of children" (Tagore, 1996, p. 506).

In his book 'Personality', he said, "In our schools, the idea of the class hides the reality of the school children – they become students and not individuals" (Tagore, 1917, Pp. 51-52). He believed freedom is very important for a student to become an individual. As Rabindranath himself put it: "I tried to assert in my world and work that education has its only meaning and object in freedom - freedom from ignorance about the laws of the universe, and freedom from passion and prejudice in our communication with the human world" (Tagore, 1996, p. 612). According to R. N. Tagore, "So, in my institution, I try to make provision for these three aspects of freedom – freedom of mind, heart and will" (Tagore, 1996, p. 508). The same opinion he made in another book entitled 'Personality', he said, "I always try to impress upon their minds that it is their own world, upon which their life ought fully and freely to react. (Tagore, 1917, p. 177). He believed that one should not limit a child to their learning, for they are born in another time because education is not an imposition but a liberal process of all-round development.

"Where the mind is without fear
And the head is held high,
Where knowledge is free.
Where the world has not been broken up into
fragments by narrow domestic walls.
Where words come out from the depth of truth,
Where tireless striving stretches its arms toward perfection.
Where the clear stream of reason has not lost its way
into the dreary desert sand of dead habit.
Where the mind is led forward by thee
Into ever-widening thought and action.

In to that heaven of freedom, my father,
Let my country awake!"

— Rabindranath Tagore, *Gitanjali: Song Offerings*

6. Teacher-Student Relationship

In conventional education, the teacher is often likened to a shopkeeper, and the student toa buyer. R. N. Tagore believed that the teacher should play the role of a Guru and that students acquire knowledge through his affection and are blessed by the glory of the teacher. This concept is known as 'Ashramer Shiksha', where the Guru deserves patience and affection for the student. The Guru should not be impulsive, insulting or punishing.

7. Educational Institution

Concept of Institution

Visva-Bharati, the International University at Santiniketan, is a combined form of literature, art and science. Visva-Bharati isa link between the East and West with universal brotherhood and international understanding along, promoting skill development in music, crafts, painting, sculpture, dance, drama and livelihood. In December 1901, an experimental school called 'Brahmacharya Ashram' was started at Santiniketan, with only five students.

Gurugriha v/s Tapoban Siksha

In the Grihastha ashram, a child learns through his own experiences in nature; attachment to nature is akin to attachment to God. In this ashram, students and teachers live together far away from the crowded city in natural beauty. As Rabindranath himself put it, "and to send me into exile, to the school, to the class with its bare white walls, its stare of dead eyes, frightened me every day. When I was once inside these walls, I did not feel natural. http://www.wbnsou.ac.in/openjournals/index.shtml pp11-17, The great task of educational institutions is to provide education of the mind and senses through various activities. Educational institutions are a wide platform where all sectors meet and forget their differences. He believed that "our university must not only instruct but live; not only think but produce." Children have active subconscious minds, and educational institutions should not be "a dead cage in which living minds are fed with artificially prepared food. Tagore pointed out that conventional education is surrounded by walls, locked gates, watched by doormen, hurried by bells, and enforced with strong punishment by teachers. Nature is the teacher for the child, and teaching and learning are possible in the lap of nature. The main objective of his, Shantiniketan, was to cultivate a love for nature, impart knowledge and wisdom in one's native language, provide freedom of mind, heart and will, a natural ambiance, and enrich Indian culture eventually.

Humanism

'Amritasya Putra' men are related to other men by nature, so universal brotherhood is the fundamental unity of humankind. He believed that God himself, along with man, is the perfect universe and education is meant for the all-round development of human personality, i.e., physical, intellectual and spiritual. Spirituality is the essence of human nature –the oneness with the globe and the oneness of the Father.

Individualism

R. N. Tagore believed that we are related to Brahman and that man is related to man. He also emphasized that as we are unique and each individual deserves freedom with his/ her inborn abilities, and each one should achieve it.

Naturalism

R. N. Tagore believed that nature is the greatest teacher and the best learning occurs in the lap of nature. Education cannot flourish properly within the four walls of a class room without effective use and understanding of our environment. Education should be imparted in natural surroundings because a teacher from nature is much more valuable than a human teacher.

Internationalism

R.N. Tagore believed that establishing a sense of brotherhood in the world would open the gates of Santiniketan and Visva-Bharati for the teaching and learning of both the East and the West.

Spiritualism

R. N. Tagore said, "Yes, it is that supreme person who has made himself known to man and made this universe so deeply personal to him. Therefore, in India, our places of pilgrimage are there, where in the confluence of the river and the sea, in the eternal snow of the mountain peak, in the lonely seashore. Some aspects of the infinite are revealed, which have a great voice for our hearts. There man has left in his images and temples, in his carvings of stone, these words - "Harkens to me; I have known the supreme Person" (Tagore, 1917, p. 45). His spiritualism is expressed in his writing 'The Religion of Man' –the spirit of religion and spirituality, God, divine experience and humanity. "Education means enabling the mind to find out that ultimate truth which emancipates us from the bondage of dust and gives us wealth not of things but of inner light, not of power but of love. It is a process of enlightenment. It is divine wealth. It helps in the realization of the truth". He believed that the ultimate aim of life is liberation from the cycle of birth and death, and it can be attained through the realization of the ultimate truth, i.e. God. Religion is to enhance creativity, which is 'the surplus in man.'

Idealism

R. N. Tagore emphasized Tapasaya and Sadhana as well as the concept of supreme truth, goodness and beauty, representing the ultimate truth of deliverance between birth and death.

Similarities

i. *Idealism:* Prof. Abdul Kalam and R. N. Tagore are idealist philosophers.
ii. *Freedom of will:* Both Prof. Abdul Kalam and R. N. Tagore believed in the freedom of will of learners in education.
iii. *Teacher-student relationship:* Prof. Abdul Kalam and R. N. Tagore emphasized the teacher-student intimate relationship.
iv. *Quality of teacher:* Prof. Abdul Kalam and R. N. Tagore emphasized teacher qualities.
v. *Quality of students:* Prof. Abdul Kalam and R. N. Tagore emphasized students' qualities.
vi. *Humanism:* Prof. Abdul Kalam and R. N. Tagore emphasized Humanism.
vii. *Mother tongue:* Prof. Abdul Kalam and R. N. Tagore emphasized mother tongue in elementary education.
viii. *Individuality:* Prof. Abdul Kalam and R. N. Tagore emphasized the individuality of students in education.
ix. *Educational institution:* Prof. Abdul Kalam and R. N. Tagore introduced a different concept of the educational institution.
x. *Development of Nationalism and Internationalism:* both Prof. Abdul Kalam and R. N. Tagore are in favour of Nationalism as well as Internationalism.

Dissimilarities

i. Prof. Abdul Kalam has the vision of an educational institution of the 21st century, but R.N. Tagore favoursTapoban/ Gristha Ashram.
ii. Prof. Abdul Kalam is in favour of Science & Technology, but R. N. Tagore – Art, Music, Drama, Science
iii. Prof. Abdul Kalam emphasised students' skill development, but R. N. Tagore emphasised village development.

iv. Prof. Abdul Kalam has emphasised material development with the manifestation of the potentiality of students, but R. N. Tagore has emphasised village development as well as the realisation of unity with God.

Summary

It entails that, Swami Vivekananda, Rabindranath Tagore and Prof. Abdul Kalam are both idealistic, Humanistic, Nationalistic, pragmatic as well as laid emphasis on freedom of will of the children. Swami Vivekananda, Rabindranath Tagore has laid emphasis on science and spirituality as well as they founded Belur Math and Shanti niketan –Viswa-Vharati as well as Prof. Kalam has given the route map of 21st century educational institution. It is also true that, Swami Vivekananda and Prof. Kalam have laid emphasis on both *kala* (art) and science but R.N. Tagore has laid emphasis on perfection of mind as well as soul.

14

Educational Contribution of Prof. Abdul Kalam

I. Educational Contributions

Prof. Abdul Kalam is an eminent scientist and philosopher whose educational contributions are important and fruitful for today's generation. His educational contributions in the present context are:

Development of the Concept of Autonomous Learning

Prof. Abdul Kalam promoted the concept of autonomous learning among students. Self-learning comes from experiences; with proper planning, self-learning is also effective in teaching-learning. All incidentals learning in life is self-learning.

Igniting the Young Generation

Prof. Abdul Kalam ignited young minds by saying that the young shoulddream, and not rest until they fulfill it. He inspired young minds to become creative and constructive and contribute to nation-building. He motivated the young generation to dream big and work hard to achieve their goals. Prof. Abdul Kalam inspired students, academicians and educators to be conscious of the mission of reconstructing the nation India by the 21st Century.

Development of Technology-based Education

Prof. Abdul Kalam advocated for the intensive use of science and technology in different courses of study. Digital libraries, practical training-based education, the use of ICT (Information and Communication Technology), intensive use of computers, television slots, and e-learning in the teaching-learning process are some of the most remarkable contributions of Prof. Kalam to education..

Development of composite curriculum: Prof. Kalam also suggested academic curriculum and skill development programme in combined form and to awarded student academic degree and training skill certificate both at a time.

Development of Leadership Quality

According to Prof. Abdul Kalam, a leader must have the capacity to envision and translate it into reality. Leaders must have the capacity to lead from the front, show benevolence from within, engage in introspection and have effective communication with people. He has emphasized the development of leadership qualities through education.

Job-oriented Education

According to Prof. Abdul Kalam, education is the prime factor for the growth and prosperity of a nation to achieve the goal of becoming a 'developed nation by 2020.' Prof. Abdul Kalam emphasized skill development and employment as the mission of education, focusing on job-oriented education.

Development of PURA and Resource Mobilization

Prof. Abdul Kalam implemented innovative methods of providing Urban Amenities in Rural Areas (PURA-Providing Urban Amenities in Rural Areas) to build up more educational institutions, health care facilities, safe water, and electricity in villages. For national development, initiatives like Chitrakoot PURA in Madhya Pradesh, Periyar PURA in Vallam, Tamil Nadu, and Loni PURA in Maharashtra, and more than 6000 PURA are relevant in resource generation and nation building.

II. Contribution to Science and Technology

Prof. Abdul Kalam developed a new education framework with the composite curriculum of science, technology and spirituality with a combined method of academic subjects and skilled practical knowledge.

Advancement of Research and Enquiry

Prof. Abdul Kalam's contribution to education includes the advancement of science and technology. He has opened new avenues for research in aeronautics, ballistic missiles and metallurgy.

Space Research

He placed the nation as self-supported in Space science through the success of SLV-III by placing Rohini Satellite close to Earth's orbit. His major contributions to education are SPACE research, AGNI- ballistic missile, PRITHI surface to surface missile, development of missile TRISHUL-surface to air missile, AKASH-surface to surface missile and NAG – anti-tank missile and Pokhran-II Nuclear Test with the vision of weapon for peace. In medical science, Kalam-Raju cost-effective coronary stent for cardiac treatment, low-weight orthosis callipers and Kalam-Raju tablet (P. C.) for rural health development is the most significant contribution of Dr A. P.J. Abdul Kalam. (APJ Abdul Kalam Contribution Towards Science, Education & Society)

Development of Mobile Laboratory

Mobile laboratory: Prof. Abdul Kalam wanted to spread information and communication technology in rural areas through mobile laboratories for school students. He started video conferences to meet officials and members of the Indian Parliament. E-learning—Web-based e-learning programmes must be facilitated to enable learning through Internet services both urban and rural areas to help the learners. The Ministry of human Resource Development has launched a programme called "Sakshat" for the same.

Summary

Prof. Abdul Kalam is an eminent scientist and philosopher; his educational contributions are important for today's generation. The educational contributions of Dr Abdul Kalam in the present context include:

i. Promoting the concept of the autonomous learner,
ii. Igniting children and youth,
iii. Promoting technology-based education,
iv. Transformation of an educational institution into knowledge society,
v. Advancement of research and higher education,
vi. Promoting the goal of education for Leadership quality,
vii. Integrating ancient and modern educational thoughts for the vision 2020,
viii. Emphasis on basic amenities of education,
ix. Education for employment,
x. Resources utilisations,
xi. Contribution in the method of science teaching,
xii. Development of the concept of quality citizen.

15

Implications of Kalam's Philosophy in Daily Life

Educational philosophy of Prof. A. P. J. Abdul Kalam has an impact on government reports of educational commissions and in our practical daily life.

National Policy on Education—1986

The National Policy on Education (1986) recommended the universalisation of Elementary Education (UEE), Vocationalisation of Higher Secondary Education, Development of technical education, Education of Girls, and Value-oriented Education. All these concepts are similar to those advocated Prof. Abdul Kalam.

Resolution of Delors Commission—1996

According to Prof. Abdul Kalam, all sorts of knowledge lie dormant in the human mind. Learning means the knowledge of hidden power from within, i.e., learning to know. He emphasized an activity-based skill development curriculum as 'learning to do'. He believed there is no difference between belief and action and whatever we think we can do. The vision is similar to learning to do. He also wanted to develop the nation of India as self-supported by the innate power of Indians as the vision of learning to be. His liberal concept of religion and practices in life is the vision of learning to live together. All these are similar to the resolution of the four pillars of the Delores Commission.

RTE Act 2009 approved the affinity of parents, teachers, students and the Government in education as it is a similar recommendation of Prof. Abdul Kalam regarding education.

National Education Policy 2020 has emphasised education through mother tongue or regional language upto class five. Educational monitory through HECL under the ministry of education, vocational curriculum from class six, freedom of the student to choose the subject from any steam with a vision 'India a global knowledge supreme power' are the reflection of Prof. Abdul Kalam's thinking.

Digital Classroom

Prof. Abdul Kalam enriched the education system by adding the digital classroom with ICT-information and technology, computer laboratory, projector and internet connection. It is much more effective now.

Defining the Goal of Education

Prof. Abdul Kalam focused on developing moral leadership quality with the development of five capacities:

- *Autonomous Learner:* Prof. Abdul Kalam introduced autonomous learning and e-learning, digital library and networking of educational institutions.
- *Development of Research:* Prof. Abdul Kalam correlates science education with its practical utility, which developed the nation with space science, missile technology, Kalam Raju Stent, Kalam-Raju Tablet, lightweight caliper for orthopedic use, higher education and research programmes prescribed by Prof. Abdul Kalam and are effective now.
- *Technology-based Learning:* Prof. Abdul Kalam suggested that the fear of "Science is a difficult subject" might be removed from the minds of children through creative presentation of classroom study with the use of laboratories and web-based presentations.
- *Science Teaching:* He defines how to teach science – firstly, the simple beauty of science is to be explained. Secondly, science teachers must be inspired to do so. Thirdly, students must be acquainted with the life and work of great scientists.

Fourthly, the value of science must be emphasised—scientific temperament developed by questioning. So students have to be allowed to ask questions and receive satisfactory answers. Prof. Abdul Kalam says that the benefits of science and its practical uses, i.e. technology, must reach rural areas of the nation.

- *Virtual Classroom:* The education system is enriched with IT technology and tale-education to enrich students' virtual classrooms.
  - *Responsibilities of a teacher:* Prof. Abdul Kalam formulated the responsibilities of a teacher – one of the education stakeholders. Now duties and responsibilities of a teacher come to the forefront of Government policies.
  - *Trial and error theory of learning:* Prof. Abdul Kalam's teaching-learning process – learning through mistakes or failure is similar to the Trial and Error theory of learning of E. l. Thorndike (1898).

Oath of the Students

i. I will pursue my education with dedication,
ii. I will plant at least five plants and take care of them,
iii. I will try to become an enlightened citizen,
iv. I will be friends with the mentally and physically challenged persons,
v. I will work hard and with honesty to develop a corruption-free nation.

Oath of the Teacher

i. I will love teaching,
ii. I will place kindness and affection before the students,
iii. I will lead by example in my life,
iv. I will encourage my students to the spirit of enquiry and to ask questions,
v. I will celebrate the success of my students,
vi. I will spread nobility of thought and action,
vii. Teaching is not just a profession; it's a passion.

Oath of the Youth

i. One has to love his/her profession,
ii. One has to teach at least ten persons to read and write,
iii. One has to plant ten trees and ensure their growth,
iv. One has to reform at least five persons from the habit of addiction and gambling,
v. One has to lead an honest life and set an example for others to adopt a transparent way of life,
vi. One has to always be a friend to a mentally and physically challenged person,
vii. One has to celebrate his country's and his people's success.

Some Life Lessons Quotes

"Be cautious of your ego that is at work." (Kalam, 2002, p. 74)

"Nation is bigger than the Individual". (Kalam, 2002, p. 180)

"With faith, you can change your destiny." (Kalam & Tiwari, 1999, p. 15)

"The best performances are accomplished when you are relaxed and free of doubt." (Kalam & Tiwari, 1999, p. 31)

"To succeed in your mission, you must have single-minded devotion to your goal." (Kalam & Tiwari, 1999, p. 89)

"Total commitment is the common denominator among all successful men and women." (Kalam & Tiwari, 1999, p. 89)

"Happiness, satisfaction, and success in life depend on making the right choices." (Kalam, 1999, p. 113)

Setbacks and disappointments have always been and always will be an inherent part of any career, even one in science. (Kalam & Tiwari, 1999, p. 123)

One should give appropriate credit where it is due; praise publicly but criticize privately. (Kalam & Tiwari, 1999, p. 124)

"What you imagine is what will transpire. What you believe is what you will achieve." (Kalam & Tiwari, 1999, p. 127)

Appendix I

With Prof. A P J Abdul Kalam*

The Modest First Citizen

I

"It was 2003. One fine afternoon, Dr B. S. Bhatia, then Director of DECU (ISRO), landed in my office at NIEPA with a few of his colleagues. Dr Bhatia told me about ISRO's new initiative of launching a dedicated satellite for education. I was thrilled; at last, our wish for a dedicated satellite would see the light of the day. This dedicated satellite, later called EDUSAT, was the brainchild of Dr Kasturirangan, then chairman of ISRO.

Dr Bhatia shared the perspective and the concept. Having heard Dr Bhatia with rapt attention and witnessing his boundless enthusiasm, I asked him, "Do you have someone in mind who can put these concepts, potentialities and plan of action in black and white?"

"Yes, of course."

"Whom do you have in mind"?

"Marmar Mukhopadhyay. That's why we are here. We request you draft the document. You have the advantage of knowing education and smattering of technology."

"Well, I do not know your satellite technology. How can I write?"

You know, education. We know satellite technology. We'll join hands. We'll write the section on satellite."

---

* Prof. Marmar Mukhopadhyay is former Professor, NIEPA, and Chairman of Education Technology and Management Academy, Gurugram (India).

The deal was done. Bhatia and his colleagues left my room after a cup of tea. I took up the assignment with all seriousness.

I signed a contract with DECU for a modest remuneration. After submitting the project report, the DECU admin asked me to raise the invoice for my remuneration. Believe it or not, I was told that night, "it's your service to the country. No remuneration." I never raised the invoice. When the DECU admin persuaded me, I told them that I had got my remuneration. Dr Bhatia, who knew me a little better, asked his staff not to pursue me.

DECU published the report under the title, educating the Nation: Need for a Dedicated Satellite under my authorship, though, in reality, the second half of the book detailing the satellite technology was authored by DECU Colleagues. After putting down the first draft, it struck me, "How about consulting the 'satellite man' Dr A. P. J. Abdul Kalam?" He was then President of India. I discussed it with Prof. PV Indiresan (former Director of IIT Madras) and one of my mentors. On Prof. Indiresan's advice, I wrote a letter to Dr Kalam's PS at the President's office. I got an appointment for 15 minutes. Prof. Indiresan was an unusual and great person. Even if he facilitated the process and spoke with Dr Kalam, he would not reveal or take the credit. On the due day, rather D-Day, I reached the Rashtrapati Bhavan with Jaya, Prof. Indiresan's wife, my old colleague and friend from TTTI days (1978), to NIEPA.

Both of us were made to sit in the President's guest room. Decently treated with tea/coffee and some snacks. Jaya was quite familiar with such protocols at the Rashtrapati Bhavan. I have visited Rashtrapati Bhavan several times, mostly on Teachers' Day Receptions. Once, I also 1 Later, I authored a book, *Story of EDUSAT* published by Shipra Publications in 2006 attended a ceremony where President Prof. Kalam received a book, otherwise called the book release function, at the Rashtrapati Bhavan.

Call came. Jaya and I got up. We were escorted to the office of the President. Jaya would have visited his office earlier, but I saw the President's Office for the first time. President's office was housed in a huge hall. In one corner, there was the President's work desk. Dr Kalam was seated gracefully, a smile flowing freely through the lips and the locks. One cannot but admire and return it with grace and gratitude. Bangla Namaste and Tamil Vanakkam (Jaya is a Tamilian) were made in concert. Dr Kalam returned it as gracefully as he was with his broad smiles.

He looked at Jaya and exclaimed, 'Oh, Mrs Indiresan, you have also come! Very Good, Very Good. I told him, 'Sir, we have known each other for more than two decades; and Prof. Indiresan's thoughts inspire me. Both Prof. Indiresan and Jaya have visited my project site at Udang'.

Dr Kalam: Do you know who is Indiresan?' Before demonstrating my great knowledge about Prof. Indiresan, Dr Kalam wrested the initiative and said, "Indiresan is the teacher of teachers; he is my teacher'. I was a little surprised. I never knew that Prof. Indiresan had taught Dr Kalam. Jaya hinted to me something. I realised it was Dr Kalam's modesty and a sincere expression of respect for Prof. Indiresan; otherwise, he has not taught Dr Kalam anywhere. Over time, I realized how well Prof. Indiresan and Dr Kalam share a mutually respectable relationship.

After these initial pleasantries, I submitted my purpose of meeting him today. We discussed for some time the EDUSAT Project. Dr Kalam gave some valuable suggestions. Most importantly, Dr Kalam said, "Professor, Satellite, and EDUSAT are all good things. But please consult some experts on packaging learning. My children must get 90% marks in the final examination; then only they can get admission to the IITs and other great institutions". I was pleasantly surprised by his down to earth approach and asking for 'packaging learning' for 'his children'. What an identification!

I said, "Sir, this happens to be my area of work and some modest specialisation. I have just come out with a state of the art book, *Educational Technology: Knowledge Assessment.* The book carries the contributions of the world leaders in the field. Can I present a copy to you, Sir?" "Yes, yes. Show it to me". He seemed impatient.

I took out a copy of my book from my bag, signed and stood up in honour to give it to Dr Kalam. Dr Kalam matched more than halfway; he, too, stood up to take the copy. With immediate curiosity, he turned over the pages. Jaya and I enjoyed watching the curious look in our revered First Citizen. He looked up and said, 'Good book. I'll read'.

'Sir, can I request you to sign another copy for me, please!' 'Sure'.

I handed over a copy to him. Dr Kalam took a green pen. He looked up and said, 'I would write Marmar and not Prof. Mukhopadhyay'.

I gladly agreed. Next couple of minutes, there was total silence. He was busy writing. He wrote something – full page. Read his writing carefully. Probably not satisfied. The smile was missing – he didn't like his own writing enough. He struck off a few words and rewrote. I noted his sincerity and seriousness of purpose with great admiration, even for such a trivial thing. Dr Kalam went back to the top of the page and reread it. The smile was back on his face. Dr Kalam closed the book and handed over the copy to me with a big smile. I did not have the patience to go out and see what he wrote. I immediately turned the book's page on my lap so that he may not see it. For me, this copy is a rare possession.

I mentioned to him about his books, particularly *Wings of Fire* and *Ignited Minds.* I liked his mentioning names of his colleagues so admiringly in his books. I mentioned, 'I happen to know some of the persons you have mentioned in your books, like Dr Pramod Kale, Sri Kiran Karnik. As soon as I took the name of Dr Chitnis, Dr Kalam almost stood up on his feet, 'No, no, no. Dr Chitnis is not my colleague. He was my boss. I have worked under him. Great mind, great boss'. I could not miss his reverence for Dr Chitnis. (Greatness of Dr Chitnis never mentioned to us that Dr Kalam worked under him).

At this point, Jaya mentioned my development work at Udang. Dr Kalam was immediately interested. I discussed briefly what we do and how it helps our village children and people. He keenly listened and asked a few questions too. His curiosity and genuine interest were far too obvious for even any suspicious mind to miss. Dr Kalam got into an engaging, relatively innocent dialogue.

'I want to visit your village and see your work.'

'That would be the rarest of luck for me and my villagers, Sir. When would you be able to visit our village?'

'But I cannot come to your village.'

I was a little surprised since he expressed his interest; otherwise, I could not have even imagined inviting India's President to my village where even walking is not easy. I mustered some courage and politely asked, 'Why, Sir?'

'Well, if I tell this, your Chief Minister will take me to his village. But I don't want to go to his village. I want to see your work'.

I realised it might be a protocol or even a security issue. I did not pursue him anymore. Let that opportunity, rather dream, pass. Innocence writ large on him; it was not a complaint, nor did he mean a Chief Minister of my home state.

There was some sound. I realised that the protocol officer was trying to signal something. I looked at my watch and realised that it was 45 minutes – our appointment was for 15 minutes. I took the initiative, 'Sir, many people must be waiting to see you.

'Yes, I know. You know it is not easy to talk to people whom I like. I need some more time with you. Can we meet sometime late in the evening so that there is no disturbance? Say around ten thirty or eleven in the evening?'

"I'll be delighted to meet you whenever convenient to you, Sir". Jaya and I stood up to take leave. Unmindful of his office and protocol, the humble man stood up, still engrossed in my village work and concern for the poor. I politely requested him not to stand up. He did not either listen or did not care. As we moved out of the row of chairs, he also moved out of his desk as if he was our equal. I felt highly uncomfortable. Dr Kalam seems to be completely oblivious of his position and protocol.

As we took his leave and moved out, many thoughts passed my mind. Most important, 'Is it being the first among the equals?'"

II
'Come, come, let's have a photograph together.'

"Prof. A. P. J. Abdul Kalam had expressed his interest in visiting Udang to see our work when I visited him in his Presidential Office in Rashtrapati Bhavan to discuss EDUSAT in 2003. I invited him. It was the fag end of his term as President of India. His office wrote back to me – far too busy a schedule, it will not be possible to accommodate this. But he may take it up later. I followed it up after he laid down the office of the President. Prof. Kalam remembered my discussion with him.

I was promptly given an appointment. I met him at his new residence at Akbar Road. I took Sabyasachi, who worked with me at the Educational Technology and Management Academy. Sabyasachi is an artist and a graphic designer. My purpose for taking him with me was to help me set up the laptop and the projector for a presentation. But he sneaked in his camera with him.

We were dot on time, somewhat before. But every other person was ushered in before us. Sabyasachi felt a little uneasy. I was comfortable; I remembered his comments earlier, 'in the office, I can't talk to people I want to spend time with. Can you come in the late evening so that we can discuss your work without any disturbance?' I had politely accepted his evening invitation, knowing that Prof. Kalam's evening begins somewhere beyond ten in the night. His Secretary wrote all his meetings marked as 'MM' (morning meeting) started at or beyond 3'o clock in the afternoon. You can now adjust his lunchtime and dinner; in case of any difficulty, you may consult '*The Kalam Effect*' by his Secretary, PM Nair.

We were called in last when all others had finished their business and gone. We went inside and realised there were no projection facilities. I set up my laptop and opened the picture presentation of my village project.

Sabyasachi positioned himself with his camera. Unmindful of urban courtesy, without

seeking his permission, he clicked. I looked at Prof. Kalam, lest he may feel annoyed. There was no expression on his face except intent attention to my slides. For Sabyasachi, it was a lifetime opportunity; he kept on clicking the camera at regular intervals.

I had designed the PPT slides as a picture presentation with very few words except for some subtitles to pictures. After a few slides, Prof. Kalam realised the technique of the PPT slides. He said, 'let me see it myself,' and dragged the laptop to himself. Prof. Kalam went through each slide carefully with full attention; no hurry. As soon as he finished seeing the slides, his first utterance was, 'I'll come to your village. My Secretary will include a visit to your village in the schedule whenever I visit Kolkata or that part of the country.' I knew that was his style; he would combine several programmes to best use time and money.

I got up. Sabyasachi clicked again. Sabyasachi asked me to stand with Prof. Kalam for a formal photograph. I sought Prof. Kalam's permission which he readily granted. As I stood keeping a little gap, Prof. Kalam asked me to come closer. I did. Sabyasachi clicked.

At this point, Sabyasachi was gesturing something to me once showing the camera, next time to Prof. Kalam. While I struggled to decipher his code, Prof. Kalam looked at Sabyasachi and said, 'Come here, young man. Come, come, let us take a photograph together. Prof. Mukhopadhyay, you go and take our photograph'. I swapped the place with Sabyasachi. Sabyasachi was thrilled but hesitant to go close to "The President". Dr Kalam asked him, 'Come, come closer, and stand here with me. His entire dialogue would give a reverse impression as if it was very important for Prof. Kalam to get a photograph with Sabyasachi. Prof. Kalam then checked with me whether the pose and position were 'alright'.

I confirmed and clicked. Prof. Kalam framed my village boy with himself.

Appendix II

Some Quotes from

*'The Kalam Effect: My Years with the President' by P. M. Nair**

"For Kalam, nothing was unimportant—everything, every scrap of paper needed to be gone into and studied. And one couldn't fool him by ignoring any papers. His memory was amazing- photographic, and with plenty of film to register information.

The following instance is one of many examples. The President was away on tour for about two days and the letters and petitions had piled up. On an average he used to get 70 to 100 petitions a day—all marked to me for MM (morning meeting). The ones that were received before he left on tour had been already marked for MM and those that were received during his absence were seen by him during his 'lunch' at around 10 p.m., after his return, and then marked to me. If breakfast was at noon. Lunch could naturally be far behind, with dinner spilling over to the early hours of the next day!

So the papers all came. I went through each one of them and as usual made cryptic notes on them on Post-its so that I could advice him intelligently on each. There was a petition from the student of ITI, Thanjavur. I explained to the President the contents of the petition and said I would forward it to the Collector, Thanjavur and ask for a report on what he could do to solve their problems. Kalam listened to me and said, 'There is one more representation.'

I said, 'No, sir, that is only a copy.' He: 'No, there is another.' I: 'It's a copy.' He repeated, 'No, Mr. Nair, there is another representation.' And I, with whom all the papers were for the past three days, and was as usual confident of my capacity to remember things, said almost with finality, 'No, sir. You were away on tour. I have gone through each of these papers. What you are referring to is perhaps a copy of this petition.' The President said, 'Okey. Let's discuss the others.'

We did, and then the files, and I returned to my room. I was rather uneasy because Kalam had said five times that there was another representation and six times I had said no. I decided to go through all the papers once again. And I froze. There was another representation from another section of the students of ITI, Thanjavur! I felt ashamed and inadequate. I rushed down to the Study and said, 'Sir, I apologize. There was another representation. You were right. I was wrong. I somehow missed it. I am sorry, sir, it will not happen again.' Kalam simply smiled and said, 'Okey, don't worry. I know you will take action on that representation also.' I retreated, feeling humbled." - P. M. Nair, *The Kalam Effect*, pp. 18-20

"...a letter addressed to him by a person from a village in Pune district. In that letter, he had dwelt at length on the travails that he and his family were undergoing because of acute financial difficulties. The letter also spoke of various illnesses that he and his wife were suffering from, the need to find suitable employment for his unemployed son, as too an appropriate match for his grown-up daughter and so on. The writer went on to say that he had knocked at the doors of district authorities, MLAs, MPs, ministers and even had written to the Government of India for immediate help but nothing was forthcoming. He was approaching the President as the last resort and if he also did not help him, the only course open to the family was to commit suicide 'en masse'.

The President was moved. He asked me what we could do. The hard-boiled bureaucrat in me made me tell him that such cases would be far too many and that if the President started dealing with such problems, there would be no end to it. This obviously did not satisfy Kalam. He said he was prepared to give the family some money from his personal account so that they did not resort to any extreme step. I advised him not to do that but said that I would write to the Collector to look into the problem and give whatever help that was possible. I would also write to the SP concerned to take adequate precautions to ensure that the family did not precipitate matters, as mentioned in the letter. Kalam agreed, though rather reluctantly."- P. M. Nair, *The Kalam Effect*, pp. 43-44

"May 2006. 'You know, Mr Nair, my relations are coming for a week or ten days. Please ensure that it is kept totally private and there is nothing official about it.' It was Kalam telling me about the upcoming visit of fifty-two of his relations starting from his elder brother who was ninety years old, right down to a one-and-a-half-year-old great-grandnephew. I knew he meant every word of what he said.

They came; they stayed for eight days. They went to Ajmer Sharif; the younger ones went shopping in Delhi too. And then they left.

Extraordinarily, not once, not even once was an office vehicle used. Specially as it was such a large number of people. Kalam paid rent for the rooms occupied by them in Rashtrapati Bhavan. Even each cup of tea was paid for by him! The bill came to Rs. 3.52 lakh, and was paid by the President from his pocket. He didn't publicize it, but I mentioned it now because I think people should know." - P. M. Nair, *The Kalam Effect*, p. 86

In October 2006, in European Parliament in Strasbourg, France, Dr Kalam delivered a speech almost 45 minutes although it was stipulated for twenty –five minutes and after that Dr Kalam said, 'I have composed a poem for you. This is from Mother Earth to the European Parliament. Shall I read it for you?' he said and he read it out.

Beautiful Environment leads
To beautiful minds
Beautiful minds generate
Freshness and creativity.
Created explorers of land and sea.
Created minds that innovate
Created great scientific minds
Created everywhere, why?
Gave birth to discoveries
Discovered a continent and unknown lands
Ventured into unexplored paths
Created new highways.
In the minds of the best
Worst was also born
Generated speeds of battle and hatred
Hundred of years of wars and blood.
Millions of my wonderful children
Lost in the land and sea
Tears flooded many nations
Many engulfed in ocean of sadness.
Then. Then came the vision of European Union,
Took the oath, 'never to turn human knowledge,
Against ourselves or others'
United in their thinking,
Actions emanated,
"To make Europe prosperous and peaceful,
Born, the European Union
That 'Glad Tidings' captivated
The people of the planet of my galaxy.
Oh! European Union, let your missions
Spread everywhere, like the air we breathe."

— P. M. Nair, *The Kalam Effect*, pp. 97-98

"In the meanwhile, he had consultations on the issue of capital punishment with legal luminaries including former chief justices of India. I remember one such occasion. Kalam was sitting with one such famous legal personality discussing the whys and why –nots of capital punishment. I was in the adjacent room since I had been told that I might be called. And fifteen minutes into their conversation, the bell rang and the ADC came to me saying 'sir, you are wanted there.'

I went in. the President and his guest were on a sofa and I sat down opposite them. The guest said, 'Mr Nair, we were discussing capital punishment. His Excellency has really clear views on it and you know them. I agree with them. What do you say?"

I looked at the President. Kalam knew what I was going to say. he smiled. "Shall I speak out, sir?' I asked. He nodded. And I spoke out respectfully, but in complete disagreement. The legal luminary was taken aback. The conversion ended and I escorted the guest out.

His car drew into North Court and the door was opened. He looked at me and said, "This is way you speak to the President of India"

'yes, sir,' I said. 'that is his strength and that is my strength too.'

He got in and the car sped off.

There can be freedom of speech even for a bureaucrat." – P. M. Nair, *The Kalam Effect*, pp. 104-105

---

*IAS, Secretary to the President, A.P.J. Abdul Kalam.

References

A.P.J. Abdul Kalam's Contribution Towards Science, Education & Society, http://recruitmentresult.com.retrired on. 25.12.2018.

Bandyopadhyay, G. (2019). Swami Vivekananda as an Educator: A Critical Study, Ph. D. Thesis submitted to University of Calcutta, Department of Education.p. 208, 216, 220

Brihadaranyaka Upanishads (1.3.28). Retrieved from https://www.speakingtree.in/blog/asatoma-sad-gamaya-brihadaranyaka-upanishad on 21.07.2018

Chauhan, K. R. (2017). A Study of Thinking on the Education System of Dr A.P.J. Abdul Kalam, *International Journal of Research in all Subjects in Multi Languages.* (IJRML), Vol. 5, Issue-8, pp. 17-22

Chakraborty, A. (2018) The Educational Philosophy of Rabindranath Tagore and Rishi Aurovinda Ghosh, *International Journal of Research and Analytical Reviews* (IJRAR), Volume 5, Issue 3, pp. 278-283

Education and National Development: Report of the Education Commission, 1964-1966 in Bandyopadhyay, G. (2018). Swami Vivekananda as an Educator: A Critical Study, Ph. D. Thesis submitted to University of Calcutta, Department of Education.p. 219

Government of India, The Report of Education Commission (December 1948-August 1949) Volume I. in Bandyopadhyay, G. (2019). Swami Vivekananda as an Educator: A Critical Study, Ph. D. Thesis submitted to University of Calcutta, Department of Education. p. 208, 209, 219

Gupta, S. (2017). Comparative view of Education: On the light of Swami Vivekananda and Rishi Aravinda, *International Research Journal of Multidisciplinary Studies*, Vol : 3, Issue-6, pp. 1-15

Goswami, N. & Malviya, D. S. (2016) Relevance of Educational Philosophy of Rabindranath Tagore in Modern India, *the International Journal of Indian Psychology*, Volume 3, issue 4, pp 69-73

India Today, (2015 July 28th) APJ Abdul Kalam's expectations from the Indian education system. Retrieved from http:// www.indiatoday.in/education-today/featurephillia/story/a.p.j.abdul-kalam on 25.12.2020

Lahiri, A. (2016). Status of Education of Scheduled Tribe Girls at Elementary Stage in the District of Birbhum, West Bengal, Ph.D. thesis, Department of Education, University of Calcutta. p. 1

Kalam, A.P.J. Abdul. & Tiwari, A. K. (1999). *Wings of Fire: An Autobiography* of Dr A.P.J. Abdul Kalam. Hyderabad: India. University Press (India) Private Limited. Prelude page ix, x, xiv, xv, xvi, page.4, 5, 6, 8, 9, 10, 11, 12, 13, 15, 16, 19, 20, 21, 22, 24, 28, 29, 31, 44, 45, 49, 60, 61, 69, 76, 77, 81, 88, 89, 97, 123, 127, 150, 151, 153, 177, 179, Back cover page

Kalam, A.P.J. Abdul. (2002). *Ignited Minds: Unleashing the Power within India.* India. Penguin Books. Prelude p. x, xi, xii, 15, 17, 19, 22, 23, 25, 31, 36, 43, 44, 67, 74, 85, 87, 89, 106, 127, 180

Kalam, A. P. J. Abdul. (2003). Teachers should be role model (on Teachers' day, 2003. p. 5. Retrieved from http://creative.snlekha.com on 25.12.2018

Kalam, A. P. J. Abdul. (2003). Teachers should be role model (on Teachers' day, 2003. p. 5.) Retrieved from http://creative.snlekha.com on 25.12.2018

http://neethuts90.blogspot.com/2013/06/thoughts-of-p-j-abdul-kalam-in.html retrieved on 10.09.2018

Kalam favours in imparting science education in mother tongue. Nagpur, January 20, 2011

Ministry of Education Government of India. Report of the Secondary Education Commission Mudallar Commission Report 1952-1953 in Bandyopadhyay, G. (2019).

Pushpanathan. T. 2013. Rabindranath Tagore's Philosophy of Education and its Influence on Indian Education. *International Journal of Current Research and Academic Review* 2013; 1(4):42-45

Rupainwar, A. (2016). Educational Thoughts and Ideas of APJ Abdul Kalam an analytical study, Ph.D. thesis of Integral University, http://hdl.handle.net./10603/114131, retrieved on May 25, 2018, p. 225, 228

Rabindranath Tagore, Gitanjali: Song Offerings

Swami Vivekananda (1972). The Complete Works of Swami Vivekananda, Advaita Ashrama. Mayavati. Vol. 4. p. 55, 358.

Swami Vivekananda as an Educator: A Critical Study, Ph. D. Thesis submitted to University of Calcutta, Department of Education.p. 214

Swami Vivekananda. (2005). The Complete Works of Swami Vivekananda, Advaita Ashrama. Kolkata. Vol. 7, p. 147-148, 170, 327.

Swami Vivekananda. (2018).The Complete Works of Swami Vivekananda, Advaita Ashrama. Kolkata, Vol. 1, p. 30, xii, 30, 412

Swami Vivekananda. (1962). The Complete Works of Swami Vivekananda, Advaita Ashrama. Mayavati. Vol. 3, P. 302, 160

Swami Vivekananda. (2005). The Complete Works of Swami Vivekananda, Advaita Ashrama. Kolkata. Vol..8. p. 78

Swami Vivekananda. (2005). The Complete Works of Swami Vivekananda, Advaita Ashrama. Kolkata. Vol. 4, p. 27.

Swami Vivekananda. (1972). The Complete Works of Swami Vivekananda, Advaita Ashrama. Mayavati. Vol. 2. p. 225

Swami Vivekananda (1993) My India: The India eternal, Ramakrishna Mission Institute of Culture, Kolkata; rpt, 2008, p. 69

Swami Vivekananda, (2005), The Complete Works of Swami Vivekananda, Advaita Ashrama, kolkata, Vol 3, p. 160, 302

Swami Vivekananda, (2018), The Complete Works of Swami Vivekananda, Advaita Ashrama, kolkata, Vol. 4, p. 27

The Hindu, (2011, January 20th). Kalam favours imparting science education in mother tongue. Para. 2

The Times of India, (2013, March 18th). Education should not be a business product: Abdul Kalam. Retrieved from http://timesofindia.indiatimes.comvretrived on 5.12.2018.

The Times of India, (2013, March 30th). Need to promote study of science, say APJ Abdul Kalam.

Tagore, R. (1917) Personality, lectures delivers in America with Illustrations, Macmillan And Co. Limited, St. Martin street, London, pp. 45, 51-52, 169-170, 176, 177, 178-179.

Tagore, 1996, p. 508, p. 612.

Tagore, Rabindranath. 1917. *My Reminiscences*. New York: The Macmillan Company.

Tirath, R (2017) Role and Impact of Rabindernath Tagore Education Philosophy in Contemporary Indian Education, *International Journal of Business Administration and Management*, ISSN 2278-3660, Volume 7, pp 150-160

What are the contribution of A.P.J Abdul Kalam in education? – Dr N.K. Arjunan http://aq.answars.com/Q/what-are-the-contributions-of-a-p-j-Abdul-Dr.A.P.J.Abdul Kalam-in-education 5/12/2018

Whatare the similarities between Dr A.P.J. Abdul Kalam and Swami Vivekananda? Retrieved from https://www.quora.com/, on 18.12.18

https://www.brainyias.com/article-21a-of-indian-constitution/. Retrieved on 10.11.2019

http://righttoeducation.in/how-was-original-article-45-constitution. Retrieved on 18.11.2019

http://www.wbnsou.ac.in/openjournals/index.shtml p 11-17 retrieved on 12.12.2022

https://archive.org/stream/ tagorehiseducati00jala/ tagorehiseducati00jala_ djvu.txt)

https://www.academia.edu/4659110/Rabindranath_Tagore_on_Education, retrieved on12.12.2022

https://archive.org/stream/tagorehiseducati00jala/tagorehiseducati00jala_ djvu.txt, retrieved on 12.12.2022

https://en.wikipedia.org/wiki/Delors_Report. Retrieved on 19.07.2019.

https://www.britannica.com/biography/A-P-J-Abdul-Kalam, retrieved on 18.11.2020

https://www.pinterest.com/pin/209065607681188265/ retrieved on 18.11.2020